Bake the world a better place!

L. Dominic

BREAKFAST BREADS
AND SWEET TREATS

FATHER DOMINIC GARRAMONE

Reedy Press
PO Box 5131
St. Louis, MO 63139, USA
www.reedypress.com

LOC: 2022937092
ISBN: 9781681063959

Design by Jill Halpin
All photos by Father Dominic Garramone

Printed in the United States of America
22 23 24 25 26   5 4 3 2 1

BREAKFAST BREADS
AND SWEET TREATS

FATHER DOMINIC GARRAMONE

This book is dedicated to my cousin Chris—travel companion, kitchen angel, and a fine baker in his own right. “Hey, batter, batter!”

CONTENTS

ACKNOWLEDGMENTS

Special thanks to:

- Our Abbot Philip, who continues to encourage my passion for baking, both by his expressions of gratitude and by his appetite for toast made of homemade bread at breakfast.
- My Stage Rats, who functioned as kitchen angels, dish washers, and taste testers for many of these recipes.
- Chef Mathew Unger, Joseph Puleo, Alvin Zamudio, and Claire Ford for their hard work on *Breakfast with the Bread Monk*, the PBS pledge special that accompanies this book.
- The staff at Reedy Press (special shout out to Barbara Northcott) for their patience with my habitual tardiness on deadlines as well as for their attention to detail.

INTRODUCTION

Are you the kind of person who orders breakfast at a late-night diner? Do you have a favorite truck stop for biscuits and gravy? Would you go out of your way to try a new donut shop, or get up early to bake cinnamon rolls on Christmas morning? Would you choose cookies over cake for your birthday treat? Then this cookbook is for you, fellow Breadhead, and for all of your family and friends who will enjoy the fruits of your labors!

When I was growing up, my maternal grandmother lived with us, and thanks to her I never left the house without breakfast. Sometimes it was as simple as what she called a "boxcar sandwich": a piece of buttered toast folded in half with crisp bacon inside. Most mornings it was cold cereal and milk, our cereal of choice being whatever brand had the best toy inside. In the days before cell phones, it was not uncommon to have a book at the breakfast table.

But on mornings when we were less rushed, my grandma would make waffles—real waffles, mind you, from scratch, made extra fluffy with the addition of beaten egg whites. I remember her teaching me to fold them gently into the batter with a red-handled rubber spatula until they were evenly distributed but still visible, with little white puffs peeking through the batter. I made them recently for my sisters and we were all transported back to the breakfast nook of our childhood home.

My mom was a champion baker as well—her breads regularly won blue ribbons at the Heart of Illinois Fair in our hometown of Peoria, Illinois—so homemade cinnamon rolls and raisin bread were a regular feature on the breakfast table. She also had an entire bookcase devoted to cookie books, and literally thousands of cookie cutters stored in large bread tins in the basement. I grew up in a house where baking was as regular an activity as Saturday morning chores and going to Mass on Sunday, with endless variety and creativity.

Cold cereal or yogurt—or nothing at all—seems to be the usual breakfast in modern times, often followed by overpriced coffees from the drive-up window. And homemade cookies seem to be rare these days, at least in some households. I hope this book will inspire you to bake your way towards a few family favorites to improve your morning routine, your sack lunch at work, your afternoon coffee break, and your midnight snacking.

Most of all, I hope you will use the recipes in this book to (as the saying goes) "Bake someone happy!" It is the nature of breakfast breads and sweet treats that we almost always make them for someone else: cinnamon rolls for family breakfast, a batch of muffins for a potluck, scones for a friend who's coming over for coffee, pastries to share with the book club or the office staff. Every holiday, religious or secular, has some kind of special breakfast bread or sweet treat, a beloved baking tradition passed down from one generation to the next. I suspect you already have your own, but I hope you'll find a new one in these pages.

God bless and happy baking!

Fr. Dominic

BREAKFAST BASICS

Let's start with some essential breakfast breads. Every self-respecting Breadhead should know how to make a decent biscuit, whether fluffy or flaky, so I've included recipes for both kinds. Bagels are easier than you think, and I'm sure English Muffin Bread will become a regular in your house. Along with a couple of other personal favorites, I've shared some instruction on the utensils you need for success.

BAGELS

Dough
1½ cups warm water
1 package active dry yeast
2 teaspoons brown sugar
½ teaspoon salt
3½ cups bread flour (see note)

Boiling
Water
3 tablespoons honey

Baking
Egg wash
Toppings like poppyseed, sesame seed, onion flakes, etc.

Place the warm water in the bowl of a stand mixer or in a medium mixing bowl and add the yeast and brown sugar. Stir to dissolve and allow to develop for 5 to 10 minutes. Stir in the salt, then add the flour, about one cup at a time, with the mixer on medium, using the dough hook. When all the flour is fully incorporated, knead it for about 10 minutes in the mixer, 15 minutes if you knead it by hand. The dough will be very stiff. Turn the dough out onto a clean countertop and divide into six equal pieces for large bagels or eight pieces for slightly smaller ones. Line one large or two smaller baking sheets with parchment paper. Shape each portion of dough into a round ball and then place them at least 3 inches apart on the baking sheets. Cover the pans with plastic wrap (don't use a dish towel because the stiff dough tends to dry out). Place the pans in a warm place and let the dough balls rise for an hour or until nearly doubled. Do not allow them to over-

NOTES

- If you want chewy, dense bagels, bread flour is best, which has a higher protein content than all-purpose flour.
- Some bakers prefer to use the more traditional barley malt syrup over the brown sugar and honey in this recipe, but it can be hard to find in some areas.
- These don't keep very well, so use them within a day or so.
- You can add just about anything to this dough: onion flakes, granulated garlic, cinnamon and raisins, mini chocolate chips, etc. I prefer plain bagels, toasted, but love flavored cream cheeses or compound butters (see page 126).

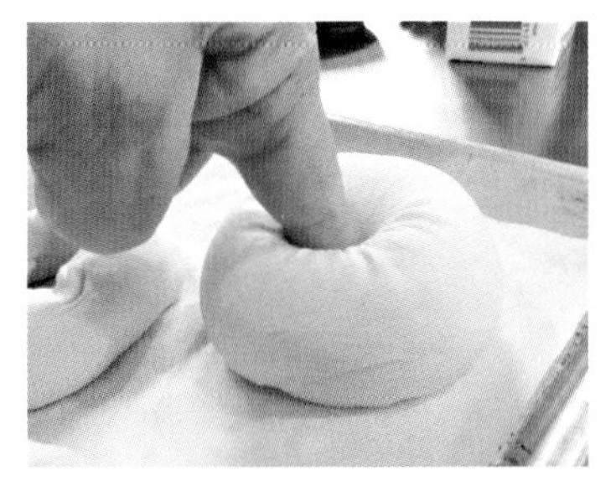

rise, or the bagels will be misshapen and wrinkly—I know this from experience!

After the dough balls have risen, take your forefinger and make a hole in the center of each ball. Spread the hole out carefully to shape the bagel shapes (the hole should be about 1½ inches across). Cover the pans again with plastic wrap while you get the water boiling. Preheat your oven to 375°F.

Fill a wide pot about ⅔ of the way with water (I use a stock pot), add the honey and bring to a medium boil. Use a spatula to gently drop the bagels into the boiling water one at a time. Boil for 90 seconds, flip over and boil for another 90 seconds. Remove and set on a clean, dry cloth or towel to drain briefly (do NOT use paper towels) and then place them back on the baking sheets. Once they are all boiled, brush the tops of the bagels with whole egg wash and add toppings if desired.

Bake for 20 to 25 minutes, or until golden brown. If you use an instant read thermometer, the interior temp should be above 200°F. Let bagels cool completely on a wire rack before slicing.

CATHEAD BISCUITS

- 2 cups self-rising flour (see note)
- 6 tablespoons vegetable shortening
- 1 cup buttermilk

Preheat the oven to 400°F. Place the flour into a medium-size bowl, and using a pastry blender, granny fork, or two knives, cut the shortening into the flour until the mixture resembles coarse crumbs. Add the buttermilk and stir until a soft ball of dough forms. Knead three or four times in the bowl to bring the dough together, and turn out onto a floured surface. Pat the dough into a square and let rest for a minute while you wipe the dough off your hands and spray a 9-inch cake pan with cooking spray. Divide the dough into nine equal portions, shape each into a flattened round and arrange in the pan (eight on the outside, one in the middle). Bake for 15 to 20 minutes or until golden brown.

NOTES

- Biscuit recipes can be a source of contention because almost everybody has a favorite version, usually based on what their grandma made. You'll find strong opinions about what brand of flour to use, baking powder versus baking soda, butter or lard or shortening, etc. I like this one because the recipe mixes up in a jiffy and makes modestly sized but fluffy biscuits.
- If you don't have self-rising flour in the house, you can make it according to the following formula: 1 cup of all-purpose flour, 1½ teaspoons of baking powder, and ¼ teaspoon of salt.

SAUSAGE GRAVY

1 pound raw breakfast sausage (pork)
2 tablespoons flour
3 cups half-and-half
2 teaspoons black pepper
½ teaspoon paprika
½ teaspoon crushed red pepper
½ teaspoon thyme (optional)
Salt

Brown sausage in skillet. Add flour stirring vigorously. When flour is incorporated into fat, add half-and-half. Heat on medium to a low boil. Add black pepper, paprika, and red pepper (also thyme, if desired). Simmer for 15 minutes, stirring occasionally, until thickened.

Taste gravy and add salt as desired.

NOTES

- This recipe comes from my friend Chef Mathew Unger, who worked with me on my PBS pledge special *Breakfast with the Bread Monk*.
- Although we tend to think almost exclusively of classic biscuits and gravy made with country sausage, there are other possibilities. Think of chorizo sausage gravy with cheddar poured over a thick square of cornbread, or Tomato Basil Scones (see page 80) topped with Italian Sausage Gravy.

BUTTERY FLAKY BISCUITS

- 2 cups self-rising flour (see note)
- ½ cup (1 stick) very cold butter, cut into slices
- 1 cup buttermilk

Preheat the oven to 425°F. Place the flour into a medium-size bowl, and using a hard bladed pastry blender, cut the butter into the flour until the mixture resembles larger coarse crumbs. Add the buttermilk and stir until a soft ball of dough forms. Knead three or four times in the bowl to bring the dough together, and turn out onto a floured surface. Use a rolling pin to roll the dough into a tall rectangle. Brush off any excess flour, divide the dough into three equal portions, and stack them. Roll out again to a tall rectangle, and repeat the cutting and stacking process. Roll out a final time to ½-inch thickness and use a cutter to cut out rounds. After the first set is cut out, press the scraps together and reroll for one or two more biscuits. Place on an ungreased baking sheet and bake for 15 to 20 minutes or until golden brown.

NOTES

- Flaky biscuits are achieved by making a laminated dough, that is, one with layers alternating between dough and butter. I put my butter slices in the freezer for about 15 minutes before beginning to make this dough, so the butter stays solid and layers remain distinct.
- For a fascinating account of how biscuits came to be a Southern staple, and about the battle between flaky and fluffy, check out *The Potlikker Papers*, by John T. Edge. He traces the history of all Southern food through the lenses of economics, politics, gender, and race.
- If you don't have self-rising flour in the house, you can make it according to the following formula: 1 cup of all-purpose flour, 1½ teaspoons of baking powder, and ¼ teaspoon of salt.

HONEY GRANOLA

- 4 cups old-fashioned rolled oats
- 1 cup sliced almonds
- 1 cup pecan pieces
- ¾ cup shredded sweetened coconut
- 3 tablespoons milled flaxseed
- 3 tablespoons wheat germ
- ½ cup honey
- ⅓ cup canola oil
- 1 tablespoon ground cinnamon
- 1 teaspoon vanilla extract

Preheat oven to 300 degrees F. In a large bowl, stir together oats, nuts, coconut, flaxseed and wheat germ. In a separate bowl, whisk together honey, oil, cinnamon and vanilla. Add honey mixture to dry ingredients and stir until well blended. Spread mixture onto two 9 x 13-inch baking sheets lightly sprayed with cooking spray. Bake in preheated oven for 10 minutes, then remove from oven and stir. Return to oven and bake for another 10 minutes, until granola is golden brown. Remove pans from oven and allow to cool completely before storing in an airtight container.

BREADHEAD BACK STORY

My mother used to make granola for our family but hers always included carob bits and raisins. I'm not much for chocolate-flavored things at breakfast apart from mocha frosting on donuts, but I do love the taste of coconut. You can add raw sunflower seeds or chopped peanuts in place of the pecans, and I've been known to sneak a few shelled pistachios into my bowl before adding skim milk. If I want to keep any of this granola for myself I have to hide it, because left on the counter with the other cereals, the entire batch disappears in about a day and a half!

PASTRY BLENDERS

Pastry blenders are used to add some kind of solid fat (lard, shortening, or butter) to a flour mixture to make a pastry crust or biscuit. Here are three tools designed for this purpose.

Wire Pastry Blender
This tool consists of a handle, usually wooden, to which stiff wires have been attached in a deep loop. It is best used on softer fats like room temperature shortening and lard, such as one might use for fluffy biscuits or pie crust.

Granny Fork
This old-fashioned tool looks like a large fork whose tines have been bent out of line, and but don't straighten them! They are designed to cut softer fats into flour, and it works especially well for Cathead Biscuits (see page 9) because you can use the tool to cut in the shortening and mix the dough: one tool, two jobs.

Bladed Pastry Blender
This more modern version of a wire pastry blender has hard metal blades, making it much more effective for blending in cold or even frozen butter, which might be called for in a recipe for scones or Buttery Flaky Biscuits (see page 13). Works just as well for softer fats like shortening, too.

Don't have any of these in the drawer? In a pinch, you can use two knives to cut in shortening or butter—it just takes a little longer.

RAISIN BREAD

- 2 packages active dry yeast
- ¼ cup warm water
- 1½ cups milk
- 2 tablespoons sugar
- 2 teaspoons salt
- 2 eggs
- 3 tablespoons butter
- 5½ to 6 cups bread flour
- 1½ cups raisins
- Extra butter and sugar for topping

Proof yeast in warm water. In a small saucepan, heat milk and butter until butter is nearly melted. Pour into a large mixing bowl and cool to lukewarm. Add yeast, sugar, salt, and egg, and stir until blended. Add 5 cups of flour, one cup at a time, until the dough is workable and pulls away from the side of the bowl. Add the raisins and mix them in by hand. Turn dough out onto a lightly floured board and knead for 5 minutes, adding enough of the remaining flour to make a smooth, elastic dough. Place in large bowl and cover with a dish towel. Let rise in a warm place free from drafts for about one hour.

Punch dough down and knead briefly to work out larger air bubbles. Form into loaves and place in greased pans. Let rise until nearly doubled, about 45 minutes. Brush the top of each loaf with melted butter and sprinkle with sugar. Bake at 425°F. for 10 minutes. Then loosely cover loaves with aluminum foil and reduce heat to 375°F. Bake for another 25 to 30 minutes. Loaves are done when they sound hollow when tapped on the bottom. Remove from pans and cool on racks.

NOTES

- This recipe has already been published in *The Breadhead Bible*, but it's such a breakfast classic I had to include it here as well. The sugar topping forms a beautiful brown crust, and the milk makes for a soft, tender crumb.
- Our Br. George of happy memory was especially fond of raisin bread, so much so that a loaf wouldn't last more than a day or so on the monastery table!

ENGLISH MUFFIN BREAD

2 packages active dry yeast
1 teaspoon sugar
¼ cup of warm water (100°F to 110°F)
2¼ cups warm milk
4½ cups all-purpose or bread flour
1½ teaspoons salt
¼ teaspoon baking soda
Cornmeal

In the bowl of a stand mixer with the paddle attachment, combine yeast, sugar, and warm water and let develop for 5 minutes. Stir in warm milk along with salt and baking powder. Add the flour gradually and mix until well incorporated: it will make a slightly stiff batter. Beat on medium speed for about 5 minutes. Cover the bowl with a cloth and allow to rise for one hour. Stir down and spoon into two medium loaf pans or into stoneware baking crocks that have been greased and sprinkled with cornmeal. Pans should be about half-filled with batter. Sprinkle cornmeal lightly over the top of the batter. Cover with a light towel and let rise in warm place for 20 to 30 minutes, or until batter nearly reaches the top of the pan. Bake at 400°F for 30 minutes—if the tops of loaves begin to brown too quickly, cover them lightly with aluminum foil. Remove from pans and cool on racks.

NOTES

- Our Fr. Ronald is especially fond of this bread and is always delighted when it shows up on the breakfast table. I have several sizes of stoneware crocks I use for this bread, but you can use canape molds to make shaped slices as well.
- This bread is actually better if served after it has cooled completely—at least three hours, or better still overnight. If you bake it at night, you can leave the loaves uncovered to cool overnight without harm—no need to stay up waiting for bread to cool. It is excellent toasted, of course. Also, the recipe is small enough that you won't have a lot of leftovers.

BAKING MIX

The first baking mixes came out in the late 1800s, but they didn't really take off until after World War II. Some baking mixes are produced for the preparation of specific foods like cakes or cornbread. The one I'm providing here can be used for pancakes, waffles, and a number of other quick breads, but the mix uses a variety of grains for healthier and heartier baked goods. A quick online search for "baking mix recipes" will give you plenty of other ideas.

MULTIGRAIN BAKING MIX

Although my mother had pancake mix and instant potatoes in the cupboard when I was growing up, I don't recall her keeping Bisquick or Jiffy baking mix around. I must confess I have never used a baking mix until just a few weeks ago when I was working on my book project *Baking Secrets from the Bread Monk* and decided to develop a recipe for a homemade version of a "Bisquick-like-baking-mix". Since then I've used it for a number of recipes, with excellent results. The one in *Baking Secrets* uses all-purpose flour alone, but here I've added some whole grains, mostly because that's how I like my waffles!

If you already use baking mixes, you might be surprised to see that this version requires refrigeration, but you might be equally surprised to discover that the Bisquick package also recommends that you refrigerate their product after opening. But most baking mixes use shortening and have a number of preservatives and therefore are more "shelf-stable" as they say in the food biz. My version has no preservatives and uses butter (far fewer trans fats), which with the addition of whole grains makes it a healthier alternative. (If you're going low-fat, use only one stick of butter.) You can use it one-to-one in any recipe that calls for baking mix.

3 cups all-purpose flour
1½ cups whole wheat flour
¾ cup quick cooking oatmeal
½ cup yellow cornmeal
¼ cup milled flaxseed
2 tablespoons baking powder
1 tablespoon salt
1 cup (2 sticks) cold unsalted butter, cut into slices

Place dry ingredients into food processor and process until thoroughly mixed. Add butter and pulse until well blended. Store in an airtight container in the refrigerator up to 6 weeks (depending upon how fresh your butter is). If you use salted butter, reduce the salt in the recipe by ½ teaspoon.

You may need slightly more milk (or slightly less mix) with a multigrain baking blend.

QUICK CINNAMON COFFEE CAKE

Streusel

⅔ cup baking mix

⅔ cup packed brown sugar

1 teaspoon ground cinnamon

3 tablespoons cold butter

Coffee Cake

2 cups baking mix

⅛ teaspoon baking soda

2 tablespoons granulated sugar

¾ cup sour cream

1½ teaspoons vanilla extract

1 egg

Heat oven to 375°F. Spray bottom and sides of 9-inch round cake pan with cooking spray and dust with flour. To make the streusel, combine ⅔ cup baking mix, brown sugar, and cinnamon in a small bowl. Cut in butter using pastry blender, until the mixture resembles coarse crumbs; set aside.

In medium bowl, combine baking mix, baking soda, and sugar and whisk until blended. In a separate bowl, beat sour cream, vanilla extract, and egg until smooth. Stir into dry ingredients until combined. Spread about 1 cup of the batter in pan. Sprinkle with about ¾ cup of the streusel. Drop remaining batter evenly over top of streusel and sprinkle remaining streusel over top.

Bake 20 to 24 minutes or until golden brown. Let stand 10 minutes before removing from pan and allow to cool slightly before serving.

NOTES

- Feel free to experiment with this recipe. You can put a layer of cake, pie, or pastry filling in the center instead of the streusel, or fresh or even canned peaches, cut into small pieces. Omit the cinnamon from the streusel, and your filling could be 1½ to 2 cups of sliced fresh strawberries, sprinkled with some granulated sugar. For a filling made with cherries, substitute almond extract for the vanilla, and toss some sliced or slivered almonds in with the streusel.

WAFFLES

2 cups baking mix
1 cup milk
4 eggs, divided
2 tablespoons vegetable oil
1 teaspoon vanilla extract

Place baking mix in a medium-size bowl. In a separate bowl, combine mix, egg yolks, oil, and vanilla extract. Stir into baking mix but don't overbeat—leave some small lumps. Beat the egg whites to stiff peak and fold them gently into the batter—there will be a few wisps of egg white visible. Allow the batter to rest for at least 10 minutes before you start using it in the waffle iron. The whole grains absorb liquid more slowly, so a little rest period will make for a thicker batter and more tender waffles, but still allow the grains to add extra texture. Use as directed by waffle iron manufacturer.

NOTES

- I have fond memories of my grandmother teaching me how to make even boxed mix waffles lighter and fluffier by separating the eggs, whisking the whites to stiff peak stage, and folding them gently into the batter. It's a method I have used ever since.
- You can add spices, mini chocolate chips, blueberries, nuts, etc. For something different, try a teaspoon of Chinese Five Spice and ¾ cup of chopped dried dates, then sprinkle the waffles with toasted pecans.

WELSH CAKES

- 2 cups baking mix
- ⅓ cup granulated sugar
- ½ teaspoon cinnamon
- ¼ teaspoon freshly ground nutmeg
- ½ cup currants or raisins
- 1 large egg
- ¼ cup cold milk
- Butter for the pan

Combine baking mix, sugar, and spices in a medium-size bowl and whisk to blend. Stir in the currants. In a separate small bowl, beat the egg with the milk; stir into mixture to make a soft dough. Turn the dough out onto a lightly floured board and knead briefly, 8 to 10 strokes. Lightly flour the board, then roll the dough to a ¼-inch thickness. Cut into rounds with a fluted cookie cutter (2½-inch or 3-inch size). Heat a cast iron skillet over medium-low heat (or use an electric skillet set to 350°F). Brush the surface of the pan lightly with butter and cook the cakes for about 3 minutes per side, or until they are golden brown. (I usually test one first to make sure I have the temperature correct—they should come out soft in the middle but not at all doughy.) Remove to a wire rack and sprinkle with granulated sugar if desired. Serve warm.

NOTES

- Welsh Cakes are a quick and easy treat, with an interior texture similar to scones but with a crisper crust because they are fried in butter on a skillet. I don't know about you, but "fried in butter on a skillet" is a phrase that always captures my attention!
- Unlike scones, they are not customarily served with clotted cream or preserves, but simply enjoyed on their own. I have heard that some people split them and spread them with jam, much like an English muffin, but the first time you make them, sprinkle them with sugar and serve them warm with a cup of Welsh Brew tea and you'll find they don't need anything else. Can't find Welsh Brew? Use Irish or English Breakfast tea instead—but don't tell the Welsh!

QUICK, EASY, & UNIQUE

Quick breads like muffins and shortcake have been around since the invention of baking soda, and I'm sharing a few you might not find elsewhere. Since they don't require the rising times of a yeasted bread, some of them take no more than an hour. Butter Pecan Breakfast Bread and Nutty Whole Grain Shortcake are my personal favorites, but bake your way through this section and see what your family thinks.

BUTTER PECAN BREAKFAST BREAD

¾ cup warm buttermilk
3 eggs, beaten
1 cup vegetable oil
2 teaspoons vanilla extract
1 cup sugar
2 cups all-purpose flour
1 package instant butterscotch pudding
1½ teaspoons baking powder
¼ teaspoon baking soda
1 cup chopped pecans
Cinnamon sugar

Preheat oven to 350°F. In a medium-size mixing bowl, add buttermilk, eggs, oil, vanilla extract, and sugar and mix well. Sift in the flour, pudding mix, baking soda, and baking powder, and beat until well blended. Fold in nuts. Grease two 8½" x 4½" loaf pans. Divide batter between the two pans, and sprinkle the top of the batter with cinnamon sugar. Place immediately in the oven and bake for 40 to 45 minutes, or until a cake tester inserted in the center of the loaf comes out clean. Cool on racks. This recipe will also make four or five mini loaves.

NOTES

- This recipe comes from season three of *Breaking Bread with Father Dominic*. One weekend when I was at our cabin at Lake Thunderbird, I decided to make this recipe. I mixed up the batter, poured it into the pans and put the two pans in the oven. I then sat down to watch PBS, not realizing that my own show was on, and saw myself putting two pans of Butter Pecan Breakfast Bread in the oven at that exact moment! I expected to hear the theme from *The Twilight Zone* playing when they came out.
- This bread is best if served slightly warm, but remember that bread continues to bake even after it comes out of the oven. Don't cut it while it's hot or the center may still be doughy. Once you're familiar with the recipe, try different flavors of pudding. Try pumpkin pudding and add two teaspoons of pumpkin pie spice to the dry ingredients, as featured in the photo. Our Fr. Alfred and I once made this same bread using chocolate pudding and chopped almonds while omitting the cinnamon. We served it as a dessert bread for lunch, and the community gobbled it up. Can't help but wonder what a pistachio version would be like . . .

PORK AND BEANS BREAD

- 1 15 or 16 ounce can of pork and beans, undrained
- 2 cups sugar
- 3 eggs, beaten
- 1 cup vegetable oil
- 1 teaspoon vanilla extract
- 3 cups all-purpose flour
- 1 tablespoon baking powder
- 1 teaspoon cinnamon
- 1 cup raisins or 1 cup chopped, toasted pecans or both

Preheat oven to 350°F. Process beans—juice and all—in a food processor until smooth. Pour mixture into a large bowl. Add sugar, eggs, oil, and vanilla extract, and mix well. Sift together flour, baking powder, and cinnamon, and stir into liquid mixture. Fold in raisins and/or nuts—do not over mix. Divide batter into two greased and floured 8½" x 4½" x 2½" pans. Bake for 50 to 60 minutes, or until a toothpick inserted in the center of the loaf comes out clean. Let cool for 10 minutes before removing the bread from the pans, then cool the rest of the way on a wire rack.

NOTES

- I often make this bread as part of a program for libraries titled "Breads Inspired by Literature." The program includes Winnie the Pooh Honey Buns, corn sticks inspired by *The Little House on the Prairie*, Victorian seed cakes as a nod to Jane Austen, and this recipe under the title "I Love a Mystery Bread."
- Your family or book club will have fun trying to guess just what the mystery ingredient is in this delicious batter bread (don't tell them about the pork and beans until they have had a taste!). Served with whipped butter and cold milk, this bread is best the next day after baking.

CHEF MATHEW'S BANANA MUFFINS

½ cup (1 stick) butter
3 large extra-ripe bananas, mashed (at least 1½ cups)
2 eggs
2 teaspoons vanilla extract
½ cup granulated sugar
½ cup brown sugar
2 cups all-purpose flour
1½ teaspoons baking soda
½ teaspoon salt
1 teaspoon cinnamon
1 cup chopped walnuts or pecans (optional)

Spray a 12-count muffin pan (see note) with nonstick spray or use cupcake liners and preheat oven to 350°F. Using the paddle attachment on a stand mixer, cream together the eggs, butter, sugars, and vanilla extract until light and fluffy. In a separate bowl, sift together the flour, baking soda, salt, and cinnamon, and whisk until combined. With the mixer on low, add the flour mixture gradually to the batter, and mix until smooth. With the mixer still running, slowly add the mashed bananas to make a thick batter. Remove the bowl from the mixer and use a rubber spatula to fold in the nuts, and to make sure you have gotten all the dry ingredients from the bottom of the bowl. Divide the batter into the 12 muffin cups and bake at 350°F for 30 to 35 minutes, or until a toothpick inserted into the center of a muffin comes out clean. Allow the muffins to cool for 5 minutes in the muffin pan, then transfer to a wire rack to continue cooling.

NOTES

- Muffin tins can vary significantly in volume, even without taking to account "mini" or "Texas-sized" versions. This recipe will yield anywhere from 12 to 18 muffins, depending upon the size of your pans. If you have the smaller ones, reduce the baking time by 5 minutes.
- I rarely make muffins, as my fellow monks seem to prefer yeast breads for breakfast. So my friend Chef Mathew Unger provided me with this recipe. I have made these muffins successfully many times, although I had to expand on his rather terse directions. Turns out my fellow monks like muffins more than I thought!

CHOCOLATE MINT MUFFINS

- 1½ cups all-purpose flour
- ½ cup granulated sugar
- ¼ cup cocoa powder
- 1 tablespoon baking powder
- ¼ teaspoon salt
- 1 egg, beaten
- 1 cup milk
- ¼ cup (½ stick) butter, melted
- 28 crème de menthe thins, chopped or ¾ cup of mint flavored baking chips

Preheat the oven to 375°F. Place paper liners in 12 muffin cups. In a medium-size bowl, sift together flour, sugar, cocoa powder, baking powder, and salt. In a separate bowl, beat the egg with the milk and the melted butter. Pour the liquid mixture into the dry ingredients and blend until the dry ingredients are just moistened; do not over mix. Gently fold in the mint morsels. Pour about a quarter cup of batter into each cup of the lined tins. Bake for 15 to 18 minutes, or until tops of muffins are slightly firm (the "toothpick-inserted-in-the-center" test doesn't always work, because of the melted chocolate in the center). Remove muffins from pan and cool on a wire rack.

BREADHEAD BACK STORY

I love everything about these muffins: their flavor and texture, the ease with which they are prepared, and the speed with which they disappear. When served warm from the oven, these minty muffins cry out for cold milk or good coffee. I had the pleasure of serving these to renowned herb gardener Jim Long at a gardeners' conference and he enjoyed them so much he asked for seconds and gave them a shout-out on his blog.

These muffins tend to fall apart coming out of the pan, so you might want to use paper liners just in case. In addition, any recipe that uses cocoa powder requires sifting of the dry ingredients as it tends to clump. Originally I used chopped up crème de menthe candies for this recipe and I still recommend them, but that was before mint-flavored baking chips were readily available. Try both and decide for yourself.

ELEPHANT EARS

- 2 cups all-purpose flour
- 2 tablespoons granulated sugar
- 2 teaspoons baking powder
- ¼ teaspoon salt
- 2 tablespoons vegetable shortening
- 1 cup 2% milk
- Oil for frying

In a medium-size bowl, combine flour, sugar, baking powder, and salt and stir to mix evenly. Cut in the shortening with pastry blender or a large fork until the mixture resembles coarse crumbs. Add the milk and stir until a soft, smooth dough forms. Shape the dough into a ball and allow to sit, covered with a dry towel for 45 minutes.

Heat oil in a frying pan on stove or use an electric skillet to heat to 375°F. Separate dough into eight even portions. Press each dough into a rough circle and work with your fingertips into a thin circle about 5 inches in diameter. Fry one or two at a time in hot oil and allow to cook until golden brown and then flip, 60 to 90 seconds per side. Remove from oil and drain on paper towels. Serve warm sprinkled with cinnamon sugar or powdered sugar.

NOTES

- These county fair favorites have their origins in Navajo fry bread, which the tribal women made using the flour, sugar, lard, and salt that had been supplied by the US government. You will also see versions of elephant ears using yeasted dough, but these are much quicker and easier to make.
- During the pandemic I gave online programs for local libraries, which included one titled "County Fair Foods." I needed pictures of elephant ears, so I enlisted some of my students to help in the test kitchen. They are, as a general rule, more than willing to do dishes in return for free samples!

FRUITED SWEET POTATO BREAD

- ¼ cup softened butter
- 1 cup sugar
- 2 eggs
- ⅓ cup orange juice
- ½ cup applesauce
- 1 cup mashed cooked sweet potato
- 2¼ cups all-purpose flour
- 2 teaspoons baking powder
- ½ teaspoon baking soda
- ½ teaspoon salt
- 1½ teaspoons ground cinnamon
- ½ teaspoon ground nutmeg
- ½ cup dark seedless raisins
- 1 cup chopped walnuts

Cream together butter, sugar, and eggs in a medium-size bowl. Add orange juice, applesauce, and sweet potato and beat well. Sift in flour, baking soda, baking powder, salt, and spices, and stir until just blended. Fold in raisins and nuts. Divide batter into four well-greased mini loaf pans. Bake in a preheated oven at 350°F for 35 to 40 minutes, or until tops are golden brown and a cake tester inserted in the center of the loaf comes out clean. Remove from pan and cool on racks.

NOTES

- Because sweet potatoes were similar to the yams of their native lands, newly arrived slaves found comfort in a familiar food. Sweet potatoes are used to flavor a variety of quick breads and yeast breads in traditional southern cooking.
- This may seem like a lot of ingredients, but the marvelously complex and subtle blend of flavors is exquisite in this bread. The aroma is so tempting that the first time I made it, the scent drew four different monks to the kitchen to investigate.
- Many sweet potato bread recipes call for a whole cup of raisins, but I think that's too sweet and overwhelms the orange and apple flavors. You could substitute pecans for the walnuts if you prefer.
- If you don't have mini-loaf pans, bake this bread in a large 9" x 5" x 3" bread pan, and bake for 60 to 65 minutes.
- As an afternoon snack, this bread is delicious served with honey butter, accompanied by Darjeeling tea or Earl Grey tea.

LAKE THUNDERBIRD ALL-AMERICAN COFFEE CAKE

1½ sticks butter
1½ cups sugar
3 eggs
1 cup sour cream
1½ teaspoons vanilla extract
3 cups cake flour or all-purpose flour
1½ teaspoons baking powder
½ teaspoon baking soda
¼ teaspoon salt
½ pint fresh raspberries or ½ cup dried cranberries
½ pint fresh blueberries
½ cup white chocolate baking morsels

Topping
½ cup brown sugar
½ cup flour
1½ teaspoons ground cinnamon
½ stick cold butter, cut into small pieces

Prepare topping (see below) and set aside. Cream butter and sugar in mixer on high until light and fluffy. Blend in eggs and vanilla extract until smooth. Sift dry ingredients together. With the mixer on low speed, alternate adding the sour cream and the dry ingredients until all is blended. Grease a 9" x 13" pan. Layer half of the batter in the pan, then place the fruit and baking morsels evenly over the batter. Cover with remaining batter. Sprinkle prepared filling on top. Bake in a preheated oven at 350°F. for 60 minutes, or until a toothpick inserted in the center comes out clean. May be served warm or cold.

Mix brown sugar, flour, and cinnamon in a separate bowl. Cut in butter with a pastry blender or mix with your hands until the texture resembles coarse crumbs.

BREADHEAD BACK STORY

Our abbey owns a small cabin near Lake Thunderbird in Henry, Illinois. It belonged to Abbot Philip's parents, but they gave it to the monastic community when they could no longer take care of it. Some monks of St. Bede use it for a spiritual haven or vacation spot, but I have used it every summer as a writer's retreat since 2001 when I was working on *Bake and Be Blessed*. Many of the recipes in this cookbook were tested in that oven and photographed on the kitchen table. The back wall of this A-frame cabin is almost all windows, so you get terrific light for food photography throughout the day.

I'm often at the cabin around Independence Day, so I developed this All-American Coffee Cake recipe to share with the lake staff who had to work the Fourth of July weekend. Sour cream and eggs give it a luscious texture, and raspberries, vanilla baking chips, and blueberries make for a red, white, and blue breakfast treat.

WHOLE GRAIN NUTTY SHORTCAKE WITH TART APPLE TOPPING

- 2¼ cups all-purpose flour
- ½ cup whole grain wheat flour
- ¼ cup old-fashioned oatmeal
- ½ cup light brown sugar, firmly packed
- 2 teaspoon baking powder
- 1 teaspoon salt
- ¼ teaspoon ground nutmeg
- ½ cup butter, cut into small pieces
- ½ cup coarsely chopped pecans
- 1 egg
- ¾ cup milk

Heat the oven to 425°F. Combine the flours, brown sugar, oatmeal, baking powder, salt, and nutmeg and stir to combine. Cut in butter using a pastry blender or two knives. Stir in the pecans. In a separate bowl, whisk together egg and milk. Add milk mixture to flour mixture and stir until blended. Turn out onto a lightly floured board and knead for five or six turns, just enough to make a cohesive dough. Divide dough in half and press into two greased 9-inch pie pans. Bake in the preheated oven for 15 to 20 minutes, or until lightly browned and slightly firm to the touch.

BREADHEAD BACK STORY

- My mom's strawberry shortcake has always been a family favorite, so I was inspired by our abbey orchard to make a hearty whole grain version to serve with a tart apple topping. The combination of flavors and textures in this treat is extraordinary: tender crumb with a slightly crisp crust, crunchy pecans, sweet and tart apples with a pinch of salt, a slight bitterness from the nutmeg. You can cut the shortcake into smaller pieces and spoon the apple mixture on top for individual servings, using small bowls or small dessert plates.
- Firm apples with some tartness are best for this recipe: MacIntosh, Braeburn, Northern Spy and of course, Granny Smith. But I've made this dessert with Honey Crisp, Gala and Lura Red apples from our monastery orchard and gotten excellent results. You'll enjoy this treat even more if you go out with your family to pick the apples yourself at a local orchard.

APPLE TOPPING

½ cup brown sugar

2 tablespoons cornstarch

1 teaspoon ground cinnamon

¼ teaspoon salt

1½ cups apple cider or apple juice

5 cups tart apples; peeled, cored, quartered, and sliced

Whipped cream and toasted pecans for topping (optional)

While the shortcake is baking, make the topping. Combine the brown sugar, cornstarch, cinnamon, and salt in a large saucepan. Stir in the cider and cook over medium-high heat until the sauce is clear and thickened. Turn the heat down to medium, then add the apples. Cover and let simmer until the apples are tender. Spoon half of the apple mixture over each shortcake layer (you may serve them individually or stacked). Serve warm with whipped cream and toasted pecans for a garnish.

ZUCCHINI CRISP

- 6 medium zucchini (about 3 pounds), peeled
- ¼ cup sugar
- 2 tablespoons apple cider vinegar
- 1 teaspoon balsamic vinegar
- 1 tablespoon lemon juice
- 1 teaspoon ground cinnamon
- 1 teaspoon vanilla extract
- ½ teaspoon nutmeg

Topping

- ½ cup tightly packed brown sugar
- ½ cup old-fashioned oats
- ¼ cup butter, cold
- ¼ cup flour
- ½ teaspoon cinnamon

Preheat the oven to 375°F. Prepare an 8" x 8" baking dish with cooking spray and set aside. Trim the stem and root from the zucchini (put them in the compost pile). Cut the zucchinis in half lengthwise and use the tip of a serving spoon to scrape out the seeds—discard but do not put the seeds in compost pile or you'll have zukes taking over your entire garden. Chop the zucchini into ¾-inch pieces. Place the zucchini pieces in a large bowl and add the sugar, vinegars, lemon juice, cinnamon, vanilla extract, and nutmeg. Stir until the zucchini is evenly coated with the mixture and pour into the baking dish.

For the topping, combine the brown sugar, oats, flour, and cinnamon (use the same bowl) and use a pastry cutter or two knives to cut the ¼ cup butter into the mixture until you get pea-sized lumps. Sprinkle the topping evenly over the zucchini mixture. Bake 35 to 40 minutes, or until the top is golden brown and the zucchini is soft. Serve warm or at room temperature.

NOTES

- There is always an over-abundance of zucchini in the late summer into fall—even if you don't have a garden! (By the way, August 8th is both the feast of Saint Dominic and National "Sneak Some Zucchini onto your Neighbor's Porch" Day!) This recipe is a great way to use it up no matter how you got it.
- In case you are wondering, no one who has tried this unique dessert has guessed that it was vegetable-based rather than made with fruit. I served it twice to our high school faculty without anyone suspecting, and my fellow monks *love* this recipe.

PASTRIES

Donuts, danishes, and other pastries are a staple of breakfast, but you shouldn't have to rely on the local bakery for your morning sweets. Puff pastry is surprisingly easy to master, and the technique will get you ready to make Danish pastry dough and the best bear claw you'll ever eat. A couple of donut recipes will provide you with a finer quality of snacks for the break room, too.

FASTNACHTS

- 1/3 cup vegetable oil
- 1/3 cup sugar
- 3/4 teaspoon ground mace or nutmeg
- 1 cup sour cream (room temperature)
- 2 eggs (room temperature)
- 3 cups all-purpose flour
- 1 teaspoon baking soda
- 2 teaspoons baking powder
- Vegetable oil for frying
- Cinnamon sugar for topping

In a medium-size bowl, combine oil, sugar, sour cream, and eggs and beat with a whisk for two minutes. In a separate bowl, sift flour and baking powder and stir until thoroughly combined. Add egg mixture and stir until just combined. With dough still in bowl, knead gently for 8 or 10 strokes. Allow dough to rest for 5 minutes, to firm up slightly. Preheat oil for frying to 350°F. Pat or roll dough out on a lightly floured surface to about 1/4-inch thick. For traditional fastnachts, cut dough into rectangles about 2" x 3" and cut a short slit down the center of each one. You may also use round or heart-shaped cookie cutters, or a traditional donut cutter. Fry in hot oil a few at a time, 2 minutes per side, until golden brown. Drain on paper towels, then toss in cinnamon sugar to coat. Best if served fresh and warm.

BREADHEAD BACK STORY

- The full name for these donuts is *fastnacht kuchen*, "Fastnacht" being the German word for the day before Ash Wednesday. There are as many different recipes for these Shrove Tuesday donuts as there are German grandmothers (the Polish grandmas fill them with jelly and call them paczki). The majority of them are made with a yeasted dough containing mashed potatoes, but I offer here a simpler recipe, easily made and best served fresh.
- Depending on the date of Easter, Fat Tuesday is often on or around Valentine's Day. Using heart shaped cookie cutters for your fastnachts is a good way to combine the two holidays. Plain granulated sugar or powdered sugar may also be used to coat them. Without a sweet topping of some kind, fastnachts can seem a little bland to the American palate, as the recipe has far less sugar than the usual sour cream donut.

DANISH PASTRY DOUGH

- 1 package active dry yeast
- ¾ cup warm milk (100°F to 110°F)
- 3 tablespoons sugar
- ½ teaspoon salt
- 1 egg
- 2½ cups all-purpose flour, divided
- 1 cup (2 sticks) cold unsalted butter

In a medium-size bowl or stand mixer, dissolve yeast in warm milk and let stand until foamy (about 10 minutes). Add sugar, salt, and eggs and stir until blended. Add 2 cups of flour and beat until smooth (about 2 minutes). Stir in another ¼ cup of flour until thoroughly incorporated, but don't overwork the dough. The mixture will be halfway between batter and bread dough—your bread baking instincts may be screaming at you to add more flour or beat it longer, but turn a deaf ear. Cover the bowl with plastic wrap and put it in the refrigerator for at least 60 minutes.

Cut the unsalted butter into slices and place it in the bowl of a stand mixer with the remaining ¼ cup of flour. Process with the paddle attachment on medium high until smooth. Form the butter into a flattened rectangle and place it between two large pieces of parchment lightly coated with cooking spray. Roll the butter out between the sheets into a rectangle about 8" x 10". Leave butter between parchment sheets and place it in the refrigerator to firm up again.

Remove dough from refrigerator, and set aside a piece about the size of a small walnut (that's your emergency repair kit). On a well-floured board or pastry cloth, roll the dough out into a rectangle 18" x 10". Peel the top layer of parchment paper off the butter, and turn it over onto one half of the dough.

Peel off the remaining parchment paper, and brush the edges of the dough lightly with water. Fold the dough on one side over the butter and dough of the other side, stretching gently to line the edges up as needed. Press edges to seal.

You now have an envelope of dough, 9" x 10", with a butter love letter tucked inside. Fold one third over the center of the dough, and use a dry pastry brush to brush off the extra flour on top. Fold the remaining third over that, so you now have a triple-decker package about 5" x 10". Line up the edges carefully and press them together. Turn the package with the narrow side directly in front of you and dust the top very lightly with flour. Roll the dough out to 10" wide and 18" tall. Fold again into a triple-decker, wrap in waxed paper or parchment, and refrigerate for 15 minutes (you now have 27 layers of butter). Repeat this process—roll out, fold, refrigerate—2 more times, after which you will have 27 x 3 x 3 = 243 layers of butter. If in the process of rolling the dough out, a hole appears and the butter sticks out, cover it with a small piece of your emergency repair kit.

Refrigerate the dough for a final 60 minutes, or overnight, and then it will be ready to form into Danish pastries (see the recipes that follow). If you refrigerate it overnight, be sure to wrap it loosely but thoroughly—I wrap mine once loosely in parchment paper that has been coated with cooking spray, then wrap it once in plastic wrap. The dough will expand in the fridge, and you don't want it to blow out of the wrapper.

NOTES

- The recipe is a half-batch version of my original recipe for Danish Pastry Dough from season three of *Breaking Bread with Father Dominic*. I halved it because rolling out a larger batch of dough to 24" x 18" is a bit daunting and requires epic counter space. This version is more manageable for the beginner and makes a more modest number of completed pastries.
- Don't let the seeming complexity of the directions keep you from trying. If you can roll out pizza crust into a circle, you can make Danish pastry. The first time I tried it, it was so easy that I berated myself for not trying it years ago.
- Don't attempt Danish pastry in a hot kitchen in July unless you are a real whiz with a rolling pin and can work quickly. The butter has to be cold in order to stay as a distinct layer from the dough. All those layers are what make the pastries light. The water in the dough turns to steam in the hot oven and forces the layers apart, and once the butter heats up, it essentially French fries each layer of dough.
- I recommend the longest rolling pin you can find, preferably a 20 inch dowel style without a taper. Mine was a gift from Gerry, a dear baking buddy who died not long after giving it to me—it's a real treasure.

ALMOND BEAR CLAW PASTRIES

- 1 batch of Danish Pastry Dough (see page 52)
- 1 12-ounce can almond filling
- ½ cup light corn syrup

On a well-floured board or pastry cloth, roll dough out into a rectangle about 12" x 18". Trim to 10" x 16"—save scraps for samples for the baker. Cut dough into small rectangles 2" x 4". Lay one teaspoon of almond filling down the center of each piece. Brush the edges with water, fold over dough and press to seal. Bend each piece into a semi-circle—the seam should be on the inner (narrow) curve. Place on an ungreased baking sheet or jelly roll pan. With a sharp pair of scissors, make four evenly spaced cuts on the wide curve of each bear claw—be careful not to cut too deep or the filling will leak out during baking. Allow bear claws to rise until doubled, 30 to 45 minutes. Bake in a preheated 350°F oven for 15 to 20 minutes, or until golden brown and slightly firm to the touch. Heat corn syrup in microwave on high for 45 seconds. Brush hot corn syrup on bear claws with a soft pastry brush. Makes 20 small pastries.

NOTES

- The first time my buddy Keith tried one of these Bear Claws warm from the oven, he quipped, "I didn't know that you knew Satan and exchanged recipes with him—these are sinful!" These little almond pastries are definitely not for "everyday"—they're a lot of work, for one thing, and very high in fat—but for special occasions, they are worth the effort.
- You may be surprised to see me using canned almond filling, but it's readily available, inexpensive, and has a good flavor, so I keep it around for when I get in the pastry mood.

FOUR CORNER DANISH PASTRIES

- 1 batch of Danish Pastry Dough (see page 52)
- Preserves, pie filling, chutney, etc.

Prepare a 9" x 13" baking sheet with parchment or vegetable cooking spray. Divide dough in half. Leave half, wrapped, in the refrigerator. On a lightly floured surface, roll portion of dough into a 9" x 9" rectangle (see note). Using a pastry cutter or a sharp knife, divide dough into 9 squares. On each square, bring the corners to the center and press down with your fingers to make an indentation about the size of a quarter. Add a tablespoon of filling to the center and place on the baking sheet. Repeat with second portion of dough or use to make some other pastry. Preheat oven to 350°F.

Cover the baking sheet with a clean dry towel and allow pastries to rise for 30 to 45 minutes or until nearly doubled. Place in the preheated oven and bake for 18 to 20 minutes or until golden brown. Remove from oven and allow to cool on the baking sheet. Drizzle with powdered sugar icing.

NOTES

- Many commercial bakeries produce very large Danish pastries with too much filling and a flood of frosting. About halfway through such a monstrosity one can feel either guilty or slightly ill! These are much more modestly sized.
- When you roll out the dough it's almost impossible to get the edges perfectly straight, so roll it out to a rough 10" x 10" and trim it as needed. I often use a vintage 3" x 3" cookie cutter I found in a monastery junk drawer. You may use the leftover pieces to shape spirals as shown, so you'll end up with a couple of samples for the baker!

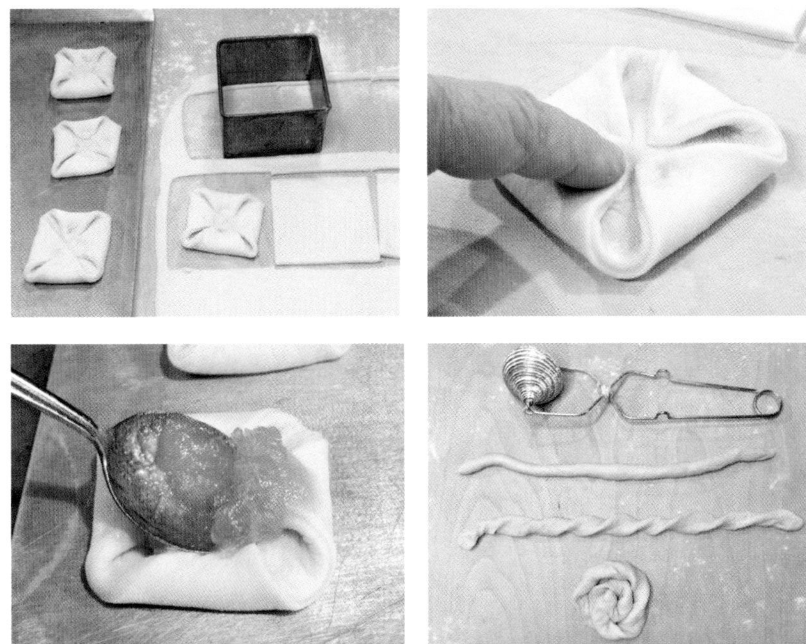

QUICK CUT-OUT CAKE DONUTS

- ¼ cup (½ stick) of softened butter
- 1 cup granulated sugar
- 1 egg (room temp)
- 2 teaspoons vanilla extract
- ¾ cup mashed potatoes
- ¼ cup milk (2% or skim)
- 2¼ cups of all-purpose flour (plus more for the work surface)
- 2½ teaspoons baking powder
- ½ teaspoon table salt
- 1 teaspoon nutmeg (½ teaspoon if grated fresh)
- Vegetable shortening or oil for frying
- Cinnamon sugar, powdered sugar, icing, etc., as desired

In a medium-size bowl, cream the butter and the sugar until fluffy. Add the egg and vanilla extract and beat until the mixture is glossy. Add the mashed potatoes and milk and beat until well blended (instant potatoes mix in easily, real potatoes may not quite incorporate all the way—no worries!).

In a separate smaller bowl, combine flour, baking powder, salt, and nutmeg and whisk until thoroughly blended. Add the dry ingredients to the potato mixture and beat just until evenly combined. The dough will be soft and fairly sticky, rather like cookie dough. Allow to rest in the bowl for 10 minutes.

Generously dust a counter or board (wood is best) with flour and turn the dough out onto the floured counter. Sprinkle the top with flour as well. Flour your hands and press the dough into a rough oval about ½-inch thick. Cut out donuts using a donut cutter (I like to use a small one, about 2½-inches across). Gather up the scraps and press them together into a ball, then flatten again to cut out more donuts. The remaining scraps can be rolled into balls to go in with the donut holes.

(Note: If the cut out donuts sit too long before frying, they can stick to the counter, or the hole is difficult to remove. I cut out four at a time, fry them immediately, and repeat until the dough is used up.)

You'll need about 2½" of oil to fry the donuts, so use a Dutch oven or a deep cast iron fryer over medium heat: bring the oil temperature up to 375°F.

A thermometer is really necessary here, unless you have a calibrated electric skillet. Fry the donuts three or four at a time, turning once: about 2 to 4 minutes per side, until browned. That may seem like a wide range of time, but a cast iron fryer, a deep skillet, and an electric fryer all behave differently, so you'll need to experiment a bit. Keep an eye on your oil temperature—if it's too cool the donuts will be oily, if it's too hot they'll be dark on the outside and doughy in the middle.

Transfer the cooked donuts to paper towels to drain. Fry the donut holes at the end all at once, stirring constantly so they are cooked on all sides, then drain on paper towels.

These donuts are just sweet enough that you can enjoy them without any topping or glaze, but you can toss them in cinnamon sugar, sprinkle them with powdered sugar, dip them in a glaze, etc.

BREADHEAD BACK STORY

I love yeasted donuts (plain glazed, thank you very much) but they require a commitment of several hours, so I can't always fit them into my schedule. Cake donuts are quicker but often require special equipment (either a batter dispenser for fried donuts or special pans for the baked version). So when I saw a recipe for a cake donut that used a soft dough instead of a batter, it quickly moved to the top of my "Recipes to Try" list. I was especially attracted to this recipe because it makes use of mashed potatoes, a common leftover in the monastery!

HOMEMADE PUFF PASTRY

- 1 scant cup of flour (1 cup minus 2 tablespoons)
- ¼ teaspoon salt
- 1 stick of unsalted butter, chilled and chopped
- ¼ cup ice cold water

In a medium mixing bowl, whisk together the flour and salt. Add the chilled butter and use a pastry cutter to cut the butter into the flour. (In a warm kitchen, you might refrigerate the bowl for 20 minutes before getting started.) Add the ice cold water and mix quickly with a dough whisk or sturdy wooden spoon. Once it comes together in a rough mass, shape it into a ball.

Flour your work surface (wood works best in my experience) and flatten the dough slightly. Dust the dough and your rolling pin with flour and roll out the dough into a rectangle about 12" x 8". Don't worry about perfect dimensions—as you fold and roll in the following steps the edges will straighten out. Using a lightly damp pastry brush, brush off the excess flour with a pastry brush. Fold the top third of the dough towards the center (like folding a letter), and brush off the excess flour again. Fold the bottom half up and press lightly.

Give the dough a quarter turn, and repeat the same steps at least three more times (I've done it up to five times for extra flaky results). The dough will become increasingly smooth with each turn. Wrap the dough in plastic wrap and refrigerate for 30 minutes to an hour before using.

NOTES

- All-purpose flour works just fine for this recipe.
- Why unsalted butter if you are going to use salt? Because unsalted butter usually has a higher fat content, perfect for pastry. If all you have is salted butter, reduce the salt to ⅛ teaspoon.
- Some recipes recommend using ice cold butter run through a cheese grater, which is fine except that I hate having to wash cheese graters!
- This makes roughly the equivalent of a single sheet of boxed puff pastry. A nice small batch for just a few treats!
- Start to finish, you can have this done in 15 to 20 minutes, plus chilling time.

PUFF PASTRY ALMOND SQUARES

1 batch of Homemade Puff Pastry (see page 60)

¾ cup almond paste or almond pastry filling

Egg wash (1 egg beaten with 1 tablespoon of water)

Powdered sugar icing

Toasted, sliced almonds

Preheat the oven to 400F° and line a baking sheet with parchment paper. On a lightly floured board, roll puff pastry into an 9" x 12" square and cut into 12 3-inch squares. Spoon 1 tablespoon of almond paste or almond pastry filling into the middle of half the squares. Brush the edges lightly with egg wash and place remaining pastry squares on top. Pinch the edges to seal with your fingers or use the tines of a fork.

Arrange squares about 2 inches apart on prepared pan. Brush the squares with egg wash and bake for 20 to 25 minutes, or until pastry is golden brown and puffed up. Allow to cool on the pan, then drizzle or brush with powdered sugar icing and top with toasted sliced almonds.

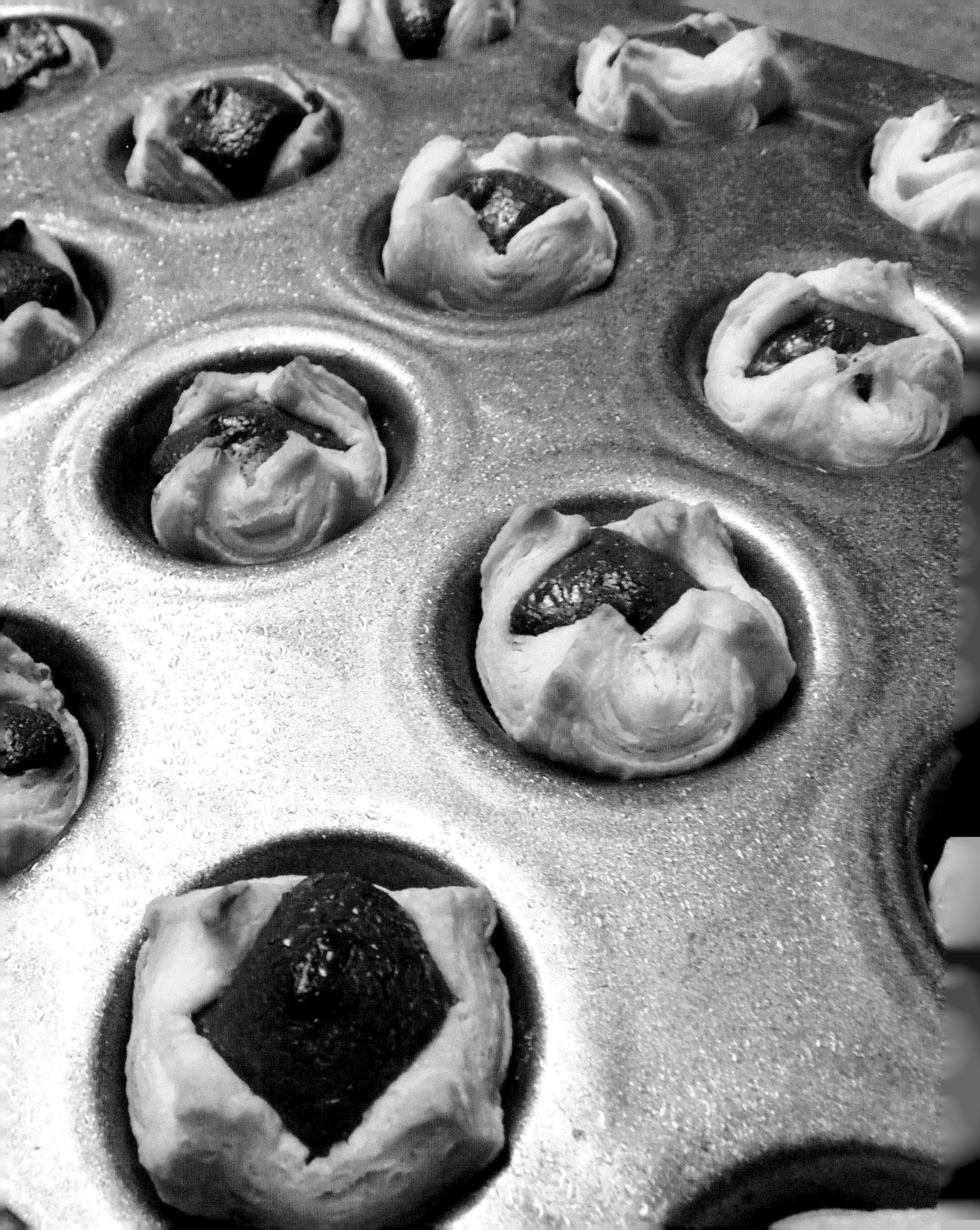

CHOCOLATE BITES

1 batch of Homemade Puff Pastry (see page 60)

24 small squares of chocolate

Preheat the oven to 400°F. Spray 24 mini muffin-pan cups with vegetable cooking spray.

Roll the pastry 12" x 8" rectangle (see note). Cut the pastry into 24 squares, each of them 2" x 2". Press each pastry square into a mini muffin-pan cup and put a chocolate square into each. (You may also use mini-chocolate chips.) Bake for 15 minutes or until the pastries are golden brown at the edges. Let the pastries cool in the pan on a wire rack for 5 minutes, then remove the pastries and let cool to lukewarm before serving.

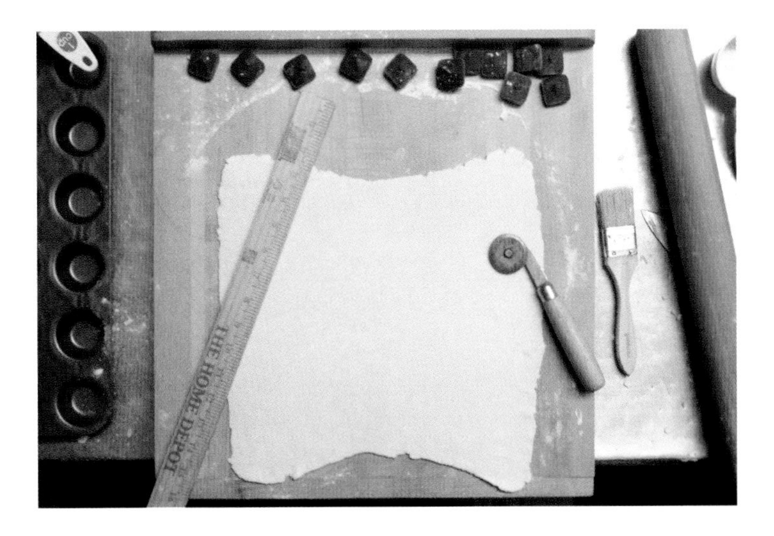

NOTES

- Unless you have superhuman skills with a rolling pin, you will probably have to roll the dough out 13" x 9" and trim the edges straight. You'll get better with practice!
- These are best eaten while still slightly warm and the chocolate is melted, but they are still pretty yummy the next day.

CHEESY EGG PUFFS

- 1 batch of Homemade Puff Pastry (see page 60)
- ¼ cup shredded cheese
- 4 large eggs
- Salt, pepper, garnish (parsley, chives, etc.)

Preheat the oven to 400°F. Line a baking sheet with parchment. You can also use cooking spray or a silicone baking mat.

On a lightly floured surface, roll the puff pastry out to about 10" x 10" and cut out four circles about 4"–4½" in diameter. Place the puff pastry circles on the baking sheet and space them about 2 inches apart. Using a paring knife, score a circle border about ¼ inch from the edge of each circle. (If you have several sizes of round cookie cutters, you can do this with a smaller cutter.) Use a fork to prick the center section all over so it doesn't puff as much in the oven. Refrigerate the pan of puff pastry for 10 minutes.

Remove the baking sheet from the fridge and place it immediately into the preheated oven. Bake the puff pastry for about 8 minutes, until the edges have risen. Remove the pan from the oven and use the back of a spoon to flatten the center section. Sprinkle a tablespoon of cheese in the center, then crack an egg into each circle. Bake for an additional 10 to 12 minutes until the egg whites are fully cooked. Remove the baked eggs, garnish, and serve immediately.

NOTES

- I love eggs in any form, and this charming breakfast treat is one of my favorites. Consider making heart-shaped puffs when you're making breakfast in bed for your valentine!
- Some people suggest that you salt and pepper the eggs before you put them in the oven, but I feel that such matters of taste are best left to the one being served.

VALENTINE BOUCHÉES

- 1 batch of Homemade Puff Pastry (see page 60)
- Large and small cookie cutters of the same shape
- Egg wash (one whole egg beaten with a tablespoon of water)
- Filling of choice (pudding, pie filling, etc.)
- Whipped cream

Preheat oven to 400°F. and line a baking sheet with parchment or cooking spray. Roll pastry sheet out to about 9" x 9". Use the larger of your two cookie cutters to cut out as many shapes as you can get out of the dough. Set half of them aside. Use the smaller cutter to cut the center out of the remaining shapes. Brush the whole shapes with egg wash and place the open shapes on top. Use the back of a knife to make small indentations on the outer edge to seal them. Place the stacks and the cut-out centers on the baking sheet and brush lightly with egg wash. Bake at 400°F. for 12 to 15 minutes or until golden brown and crisp. Cool on the pan.

Fill the bouchées with:

- Cheesecake flavored pudding, cherry pie filling, and a dollop of whipped cream
- Layers of marshmallow crème and fudge sauce
- Diced pears sprinkled with Chinese Five Spice and toasted pecans
- Fresh berries and clotted cream

The cut-out centers may be used as a garnish.

SCONES

Mention scones in a group of foodies and someone will inevitably say, "Scones are always so dry and tough." Any Breadhead in the group will reply indignantly, "Not *my* scones!" Once you learn how to make your own scones, you'll never again settle for a dried-out scone from the coffee shop case. You might be surprised to discover that there are savory scones as well: Tomato Basil Scones with Italian Sausage Gravy is a meal for *any* time of day!

BACON CHEDDAR CHIVE SCONES

- 2 cups all-purpose flour
- 2 teaspoons sugar
- 2 teaspoons baking powder
- 1 teaspoon baking soda
- ½ teaspoon salt
- ½ cup (one stick) cold butter
- 1 cup shredded cheddar cheese
- ½ cup minced fresh chives
- 8 ounces bacon, cooked crisp and chopped (about 1 cup)
- 1 cup sour cream

Preheat the oven to 425°F. Lightly grease a 9" x 13" baking sheet and set aside. Place flour, sugar, baking powder, baking soda, and salt in a medium-size bowl and whisk together until blended. Work the butter into the flour with a pastry cutter until the mixture resembles coarse bread crumbs. Add cheese, chives, and bacon and stir till evenly distributed. Add sour cream and mix until a cohesive ball of dough is formed; do not over-mix.

Transfer the dough to a well-floured work surface. Pat or roll the dough into an 8-inch disk about ¾-inch thick. Use a chef's knife, bench knife, or large pizza cutter to cut the disk into eight wedges. Transfer wedges to the prepared pan, evenly spaced. You may also use a divided cast iron skillet. Bake the scones for 20 to 25 minutes, until golden brown. Cool on the pan and serve warm.

NOTES

- This recipe was my first attempt at a savory scone, and it took a few tries to get the flavor profile just right. The cheese adds not only flavor but make for a crunchier crust on the outside and a more tender crumb on the inside. As you can see from the photo, you can use a segmented cast-iron pan (usually used for corn bread) to get even more crunch on the edges.

CHOCOLATE MINT SCONES

- 2 cups all-purpose flour
- 1 tablespoon baking powder
- 1 tablespoon granulated sugar, plus more for topping
- ½ teaspoon salt
- 1 stick cold butter, cut into small pieces
- 1 cup chopped chocolate mint candies
- ½ cup sweet cream (plus more for brushing tops)
- 2 eggs

Pre-heat the oven to 400°F. and place the cut-up butter in the freezer while you assemble the other ingredients. Having cold sour cream and eggs is essential the success of this recipe as well. In a large bowl, combine flour, baking powder, sugar, and salt and whisk until well-blended. Add the pieces of butter and cut them in using a pastry cutter or two forks (a pastry cutter with hard blades instead of wire loops works better) until the mixture resembles coarse crumbs. Stir in the chopped mint candies. In a separate container, whisk together sour cream and eggs, then pour into the flour and butter mixture. Stir until the dough comes together in a loose ball, then turn out onto the countertop and knead gently to incorporate all the stray bits. Do not over-knead.

Roll or pat the dough into an 8-inch circle and divide into eight wedges with a sharp knife or a rotary pizza cutter. Place the wedges slightly separate from each other on a baking sheet lined with parchment, or on a 12-inch pizza pan coated with cooking spray. Brush the tops lightly with cream and sprinkle with granulated sugar. Place immediately in the oven and bake for 15 to 18 minutes or until golden brown. If it's hot in the kitchen, place the scones on their pan in the refrigerator for 10 to 15 minutes before baking to prevent them from spreading out too much. This step isn't necessary if your dough remains chilled.

These scones are lightly sweet and not at all heavy, but you might want to dress them up with a little drizzle of chocolate. Place 2 tablespoons of chocolate chips into a small plastic bag and microwave in 10 second increments until melted. Snip the corner of the bag with a sharp pair of scissors and drizzle away. I put 2 tablespoons each of powdered sugar and cocoa powder into a Pyrex pitcher with teaspoon or two of milk and a tablespoon of chopped candies, and popped it in the microwave for 10 to 15 seconds. A quick stir with a fork and it was ready to drizzle.

NORFOLK SCONES

- 1 batch of Classic Scone dough (see page 78)
- ½ cup cherry preserves or cake filling

Preheat oven to 400°F. Prepare a baking sheet or pizza pan with cooking spray. Divide dough in half and pat one section of dough into an 8-inch circle in the center of the baking sheet (it helps to butter your hands so the dough will not stick to you). Spread the filling evenly over the circle of dough. Spray a piece of parchment lightly with cooking spray, and pat the second portion of dough into an 8-inch circle. Carefully flip the second circle of dough on top of the first and peel off the parchment paper. Using a large knife or rotary pizza cutter, divide dough into eight wedges, but leave the outer ¼ inch of the circle uncut, so the wedges stay together during baking. Wipe the knife or pizza cutter clean after each cut.

Bake at 400°F for 15 to 20 minutes, or until round is firm on the edges but still slightly soft in the middle. Cool on a wire rack, then cut apart before serving. You can also top these with a light drizzle of icing (see page 130).

NOTES

- Norfolk scones traditionally have a filling of currants, butter, spices, and turbinado sugar. I prefer a fruit preserve filling, in part because of the beautiful look of the layers. You can use pretty much any flavor of preserve or cake filling you want, but I'm fond of sour cherry preserves. If you use blueberry filling, add a little lemon zest to the drizzle.
- I have some dear friends who often vacation in Michigan and bring me back preserves made with the state's fruits: sour cherries, Bartlett pears, strawberries, blueberries, etc. Pretty much every one of these flavors have gone into a Norfolk scone recipe!

CLASSIC SCONES

- 2 cups all-purpose flour
- 1 tablespoon baking powder
- 3 tablespoons granulated sugar, plus more for topping
- ½ teaspoon salt
- 4 tablespoons (½ stick) cold butter, cut into small pieces
- ½ cup cream (plus more for brushing tops)
- 2 eggs
- 1 teaspoon vanilla extract

Pre-heat the oven to 400°F. and place the cut-up butter in the freezer while you assemble the other ingredients. Having cold cream and eggs is essential the success of this recipe as well. In a large bowl, combine flour, baking powder, sugar, and salt and whisk until well-blended. Add the pieces of butter and cut them in using a pastry cutter or two forks (a pastry cutter with hard blades instead of wire loops works better) until the mixture resembles coarse crumbs. In a separate container, whisk together cream, eggs, and vanilla extract, then pour into the flour and butter mixture. Stir until the dough comes together in a loose ball, then turn out onto the countertop and knead gently to incorporate all the stray bits. Do not over-knead.

Roll or pat the dough into an 8-inch circle and divide into eight wedges with a sharp knife or a rotary pizza cutter. Place the wedges slightly separate from each other on a baking sheet lined with parchment, or on a 12-inch pizza pan coated with cooking spray. Brush the tops lightly with cream and sprinkle with granulated sugar. Place immediately in the oven and bake for 15 to 18 minutes or until golden brown. If it's hot in the kitchen, place the scones on their pan in the refrigerator for 10 to 15 minutes before baking to prevent them from spreading out too much. This step isn't necessary if your dough remains chilled.

COFFEEHOUSE CINNAMON SCONES

- 2 cups all-purpose flour
- 2 teaspoons baking powder
- ¼ cup granulated sugar
- ½ teaspoon salt
- ½ teaspoon cinnamon
- ¼ teaspoon nutmeg
- 1 stick cold butter, cut into small pieces
- ¾ cinnamon baking chips
- ½ cup cream (plus more for brushing tops)
- 2 eggs
- 1 teaspoon vanilla extract
- 2 tablespoons demerara or turbinado sugar

Pre-heat the oven to 375°F. and place the cut-up butter in the freezer while you assemble the other ingredients. Having cold cream and eggs is essential the success of this recipe as well. In a large bowl, combine flour, baking powder, sugar, salt, cinnamon, and nutmeg, and whisk until well-blended. Add the pieces of butter and cut them in using a pastry cutter or two forks (a pastry cutter with hard blades instead of wire loops works better) until the mixture resembles coarse crumbs. In a separate container, whisk together cream, eggs, and vanilla extract, then pour into the flour and butter mixture. Stir until the dough comes together in a loose ball, then turn out onto the countertop and knead gently to incorporate all the stray bits. Do not over-knead.

Roll or pat the dough into an 8-inch circle and divide into eight wedges with a sharp knife or a rotary pizza cutter. Place the wedges slightly separate from each other on a baking sheet lined with parchment, or on a 12-inch pizza pan coated with cooking spray. Brush the tops lightly with cream and sprinkle with demerara sugar. Place immediately in the oven and bake for 15 to 18 minutes or until golden brown. If it's hot in the kitchen, place the scones on their pan in the refrigerator for 10 to 15 minutes before baking to prevent them from spreading out too much. This step isn't necessary if your dough remains chilled.

TOMATO BASIL SCONES

- 2 cups all-purpose flour
- 2 tablespoons sugar
- 2 teaspoons baking powder
- ½ teaspoon baking soda
- ½ teaspoon salt
- ¼ cup (½ stick) cold butter cut into slices
- 2 tablespoons minced fresh basil (2 teaspoons dried)
- 2 tablespoons minced fresh parsley (1 tablespoon dried)
- ½ teaspoon minced fresh rosemary (¼ teaspoon dried and ground)
- ½ cup chopped sun-dried tomatoes (not in oil)
- ¾ cup crushed tomatoes
- Garlic butter and parmesan for topping (optional)

Preheat oven to 425°F. and lightly grease an 8" x 8" cake pan. In a medium-size bowl, whisk together flour, sugar, baking powder, baking soda, and salt. Cut in butter with a pastry blender or two knives until mixture resembles coarse crumbs. Stir in herbs and sun-dried tomatoes until evenly distributed. Add crushed tomatoes and mix until dough forms into a ball. Knead gently for five or six strokes. Press dough into pan until spread evenly in pan. Using a bench knife or spatula, divide into nine squares. Bake for 20 to 25 minutes or until browned and the scones are slightly firm to the touch. Allow to cool in pan for 10 minutes before serving warm. If desired, brush with melted garlic butter and Parmesan cheese before serving.

BREADHEAD BACK STORY

As soon as there's fresh basil in our kitchen garden, I want to make tomato dishes. The brethren gobbled up these savory scones the first time I served them. Try them smothered in Italian Sausage Gravy for breakfast. If you're serving them with soup later in the day, by all means use the garlic butter and Parmesan topping.

My first attempt at this recipe included some shredded zucchini, since I had some monster squash to use up. The zucchini added too much liquid and almost no flavor, so I abandoned it in scones and stuck to walnut zucchini batter bread from then on! It's unusual for a scone recipe not to include some kind of dairy for the liquid, so you may find the texture a little off-putting at first, but the flavor is exquisite.

It may seem a bit odd to make scones in a square cake pan, but the dough is easier to manage that way and makes for neat and even servings. They are also modestly sized, in contrast to the giant wedges you see in some coffee shops. If you make it as a scored round on a baking sheet like traditional scones, reduce the baking time to about 20 minutes.

STRAWBERRY CREAM SCONES

2 cups all-purpose flour
2 teaspoons sugar
2 teaspoons baking powder
½ teaspoon salt
6 tablespoons cold butter
1 cup chopped strawberries (¼ inch dice)
¾ cup heavy cream

Preheat the oven to 425°F. Lightly grease a 9" x 13" baking sheet and set aside. Place flour, sugar, baking powder, baking soda, and salt in a medium-size bowl and whisk together until blended. Work the butter into the flour with a pastry cutter until the mixture resembles coarse bread crumbs. Add strawberries and stir till evenly distributed. Add cream and mix until a cohesive ball of dough is formed; do not over-mix.

Transfer the dough to a well-floured work surface. Pat or roll the dough into an 8-inch disk about ¾-inch thick. Use a chef's knife, bench knife, or large pizza cutter to cut the disk into eight wedges. (You may also use a round or heart-shaped cookie cutter.) Transfer scones to the prepared pan, evenly spaced. Bake the scones for 20 to 25 minutes, until golden brown. Cool on the pan and serve warm.

BREADHEAD BACK STORY

When I was in "the scone phase" of recipe testing, I discovered that we had several pints of fresh strawberries that needed to be used up pretty quickly. As a practical baker, I thought that was reason enough to make these classic scones. Strawberries and cream go together, and the richness of the cream means you can use a little less butter on this recipe. In a convection oven (with the blower on), there's real risk of the strawberries on the surface of the dough getting scorched black, so if you are using one be sure to cover the pan lightly with aluminum foil until the last few minutes of baking. The strawberry flavor of these scones is rather delicate, so don't serve them with an overwhelmingly strong coffee or heavily flavored tea—for the latter, I recommend Formosa Oolong.

This is a fairly classic scone recipe, and you could substitute raisins, dried cranberries, or blueberries with equally delightful results. I like to use dried apricots or snipped dates with chopped pecans and serve them with clotted cream and a little spoonful of orange marmalade. When I tested the recipe, this strawberry version was enjoyed both by the monks at breakfast and some of the faculty at lunch, and the only criticism I received was that I hadn't made enough for the whole staff!

YEASTED BREADS

Many people tell me that they are afraid of yeast bread recipes, in part because they lack kneading skills. But now that stand mixers with a dough hook are a more common feature in kitchens, more and more beginner bakers are finding success. My versatile Sour Cream Sweet Dough is a good place to start. Then move on to a couple of ethnic breads from Greece and Scotland, respectively. Warning: don't look at the photos too late in the evening or you'll be up all night baking!

SOUR CREAM SWEET DOUGH

½ cup warm water
1 package active dry yeast
½ cup sour cream
¼ cup sugar
1 egg
¼ cup (½ stick) of butter melted and cooled to lukewarm
½ teaspoon salt
½ teaspoon vanilla extract
3½ cups of all-purpose flour

Place warm water in bowl of stand mixer and stir in yeast. Allow to dissolve and get foamy, about 10 minutes. In a separate container, warm the sour cream and stir in the sugar until dissolved (make sure it's only lukewarm or you'll scramble the egg in the next step!). Add the egg, melted butter, salt, and vanilla extract, and whisk until smooth. Add the sour cream mixture to the yeast mixture and beat until smooth—use the paddle attachment.

Add one cup of flour and stir until thoroughly incorporated. Repeat with a second cup of flour. Switch to the dough hook attachment, and gradually add the remaining flour, a little at a time, to make a soft dough that is rather sticky. Knead with the dough hook for about 6 minutes. The dough will be softer than most bread doughs, but still smooth and elastic. Place dough back in the rinsed bowl, cover with a dry towel, and let rise in a warm place free from drafts until doubled in bulk, 60 to 75 minutes. Proceed as directed for shaping.

NOTES

- This recipe may be done by hand instead of in a stand mixer, but it's a soft, somewhat sticky dough and I find that the stand mixer does a better job.
- With such a rich dough, both the first and second rises may take a little longer than usual—be patient!

GLAZED DONUTS

1 batch of Sour Cream Sweet Dough (see page 86)

Glaze

2 cups sifted powdered sugar

½ teaspoon vanilla extract

⅓ cup warm water

Roll out dough on a floured board to a thickness of ½ inch. Use a donut cutter to cut out donuts and holes and place them on a well-oiled baking sheet. Scraps may be kneaded together briefly and rolled out a second time. Allow donuts and holes to rise, covered with a dry cloth, for 25 to 30 minutes or until nearly doubled. Fry two or three donuts at a time in 375°F oil until golden brown, about 2 minutes per side (I flip mine with a pair of chopsticks). Drain on paper towels and allow to cool slightly. Glaze while still warm. Makes about a dozen donuts and donut holes.

Glaze

Stir until smooth, then dip donuts in glaze one at a time, turning to coat completely. Set on wire racks to allow excess to drip off, then serve.

BREADHEAD BACK STORY

- My favorite glazed donuts, bar none, were the ones served at the Mr. Donut on Knoxville Avenue in Peoria. I remember looking through the window between the serving area and kitchen and watching the baker roll out huge sheets of soft dough and cut out the donuts with a well-used cutter. As he cut each donut, he would flip it onto his thumb with a flick of his wrist and the hole would pop out. He'd cut and collect four or five donuts this way and then lay them out on the wire rack to rise. Several years ago I bought a professional donut cutter at a flea market, but I've yet to master his "flick" technique!
- As a general rule it's easiest to make donuts in an electric fryer with a thermostat to keep the temperature both accurate and constant, but if you have some experience frying in a large cast iron skillet with deep sides, you'll have no problem with that method. Use a clip-on candy thermometer to keep track of the oil temperature.

LEMON FANTANS

1 batch of Sour Cream Sweet Dough (see page 86)

Lemon Filling

½ cup granulated sugar

3 tablespoons grated lemon zest

2 or 3 lemons (depending on size)

3 tablespoons butter, melted

Icing

1 cup powdered sugar

1 tablespoon milk

2 tablespoons lemon juice

Gently deflate the dough—do not punch down and knead, or you will have to let it rest 10 minutes before rolling it out. On a lightly floured board, roll out the dough into a rectangle, about 20" x 12". Using a soft pastry brush, spread the melted butter over the dough. Starting from the long side, use a small pizza cutter or pastry wheel to cut the dough into 10 equal strips, each about 2" x 12".

Lightly grease a 12-cup muffin tin. Sprinkle about 2 teaspoons of the zest-sugar mixture over one strip of dough (press sugar mixture in gently, so it doesn't fall off when you move the stack later). Top with a second strip and sprinkle it with the zest-sugar mixture. Repeat with two more sections and then top with a final strip of dough. Repeat procedure, so that you end up with two stacks of five strips.

BREADHEAD BACK STORY

Butter fantans are an old-fashioned dinner roll you don't see anymore, but they served as the inspiration for these lemony breakfast treats. My first experiment with this recipe was in the form of a large pull-apart loaf, but I thought it was awkward to serve in that form. A muffin-sized roll is easier to serve and eat.

After developing this recipe while at Lake Thunderbird, I took some to the local fire station for the late shift and was greeted with enthusiastic gratitude. Whenever you see a recipe that appeals to you—in this book or on Pinterest or in a magazine—think seriously about sharing your goodies with local police, EMTs, ER nurses, and other service personnel.

Using a very sharp knife, slice the stack crosswise through the five layers to create 12 sections, each about 2" x 2". Place each stack into a muffin cup cut edges up (you may have to squish them a bit). Cover with a clean, dry cloth and let rise in a warm place free of drafts until nearly doubled, about 30 minutes.

Preheat oven to 350°F. Bake on the middle rack until the top is golden brown, 15 to 20 minutes. Transfer pan to a wire rack and let cool in the pan for 10 minutes before removing rolls. In a medium bowl, whisk milk and lemon juice with powdered sugar until the mixture is smooth. Drizzle over rolls and serve warm.

OVERNIGHT CINNAMON ROLLS

- 1 batch of Sour Cream Sweet Dough (see page 86)
- 1 tablespoon butter, melted
- ½ cup granulated sugar
- ¼ cup light brown sugar
- 1 tablespoon cinnamon

Spray a 9" x 9" baking pan with cooking spray and set aside. In a small bowl, whisk the granulated sugar, brown sugar, and cinnamon together and set aside. Gently remove the proofed dough from its bowl—do not punch down or knead—and place it on a floured countertop. With your hands, flatten it slightly and shape it roughly into a rectangle. Sprinkle flour on the top of the dough and on your rolling pin, and roll the dough into a rectangle about 14" x 10"—you may need to re-flour the counter and/or the surface of the dough as you work. Since you didn't deflate the dough or knead it, it should roll out easily. Leaving a ½-inch border of "clean dough" on the top shorter edge, brush on the melted butter over the rest of dough and sprinkle on the sugar mixture. Brush a little water on the top edge. Starting with the shorter edge, roll dough up tightly and pinch to seal the seam. Using a sharp knife, cut into nine equal slices and place them cut side up, evenly spaced in the prepared pan. Cover the pan tightly with plastic wrap and refrigerate overnight, or up to 12 hours.

When you're ready to bake, remove the rolls from the refrigerator and take off the plastic wrap. They may not appear that much different than when you put them in, but fear not—we just need to wake the yeast back up. Fill a 9" x 13" pan about ⅔ full of boiling water and set on the lower rack of an *unheated* oven. Place the rolls on the middle rack,

close the oven door and let the rolls rise until they are nearly doubled, which can take anywhere from 30 to 60 minutes. (If your kitchen is cold, replace the hot water half way through.) Remove both the rolls and the shallow pan of water from the oven.

Preheat the oven to 350°F. Bake the rolls on the middle rack for 25 to 30 minutes. The interior temperature of the rolls should be 190°F to 195°F. Cool in the pan on a wire rack. Cool to lukewarm and top with either drizzle or cream cheese frosting (see page 130).

NOTES

- I must confess, I have never had much use for an overnight cinnamon rolls recipe and could never understand why anyone would go to all that trouble. But then I realized—monks never sleep in! Morning prayer is at 5:45 a.m., with breakfast to follow, so I'd have to get up at 3:30 a.m. or so to get these out in time for prayers! But if you are the early riser on most weekend mornings and everyone else sleeps in until 9:00 a.m., then you may enjoy having this recipe on hand. Some people have told me it's a Christmas morning tradition for their families.
- The Sour Cream Sweet Dough is very rich, which slows down the rising process considerably. If you use a basic dinner roll dough, things will move along a little more quickly.

STRAWBERRY BREAKFAST ROLLS

- 1 batch of Sour Cream Sweet Dough (see page 86)
- 1 cup water
- 3 tablespoons cornstarch
- 2½ cups fresh strawberries, cut into bite size pieces
- ¾ cup white sugar
- 1 tablespoon lemon juice

While your dough is proofing, make the strawberry filling. Whisk water and cornstarch together in a medium saucepan. Stir strawberries, sugar, and lemon juice into the water. Cook strawberry mixture over medium heat, stirring occasionally, until the mixture is thick, about 10 minutes. Allow to cool completely before use.

Prepare a 9" x 9" with vegetable cooking spray and place a square of parchment on the bottom of the pan. After the dough is fully proofed, remove it from its bowl—do not punch down or knead—and place it on a floured countertop. With your hands, flatten it slightly and shape it roughly into a rectangle. Sprinkle flour on the top of the dough and on your rolling pin, and roll the dough into a rectangle about 14" x 10"—you may need to re-flour the counter and/or the surface of the dough as you work. Since you didn't deflate the dough or knead it, it should roll out easily. Leaving a ½-inch border of "clean dough" on all sides, spread the strawberry filling evenly over the dough. Brush a little water on the top edge so it will stick. Starting with the

NOTES

- I first made these many years ago when strawberries went on deep discount at the local grocery store because they were nearly overripe. I bought quite a few quarts and made preserves, strawberry rhubarb pie, and then created this filling as a topping for waffles. But it occurred to me that it might make a lovely filling for breakfast rolls as well. The brethren were grateful for the inspiration!

shorter edge, roll dough up tightly and pinch to seal the seam. Using a sharp knife, cut into nine equal slices and place them cut side up, evenly spaced in the prepared pan. Cover with a dry towel and allow to rise for 30 to 45 minutes.

When they are nearly doubled, preheat the oven to 350°F. Bake the rolls on the middle rack for 25 to 30 minutes. Cool in the pan on a wire rack for about half an hour before removing them (the parchment keeps the strawberry filling from burning and fusing to the pan!). Top with drizzle or cream cheese frosting (see page 130).

SWEETHEART COFFEE CAKE

- 1 batch of Sour Cream Sweet Dough (see page 86)
- 1 (12 ounce) can cherry or raspberry pastry filling
- Powdered Sugar Drizzle (see page 130)
- Sliced almonds (optional)

On a lightly floured board, roll dough out into a rectangle 12" x 14". Spread the filling over the dough, leaving 1 inch of the top wide edge dry. Starting at the bottom wide edge, roll the dough up jelly roll style. Lightly brush the top edge with a little water, so it will stick to the roll; pinch to seal. Using a sharp knife cut the roll lengthwise, leaving about 2 inches uncut at both ends. Grasp the two sections near the top and rotate them so the interior layers are facing upwards, and pull the top section toward you to form the heart shape (see photos). Place on a baking sheet or jelly roll pan lined with parchment. Cover with a dry towel and let rise until doubled, 30 to 45 minutes. Bake in a preheated 375°F oven for 20 to 25 minutes or until lightly browned. Remove from baking sheet and cool on rack. Decorate with swirls of Powdered Sugar Drizzle and sprinkle with toasted sliced almonds if desired.

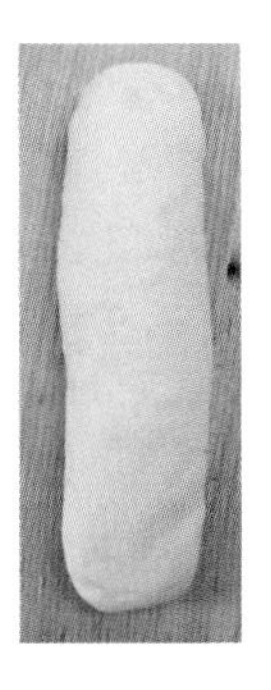
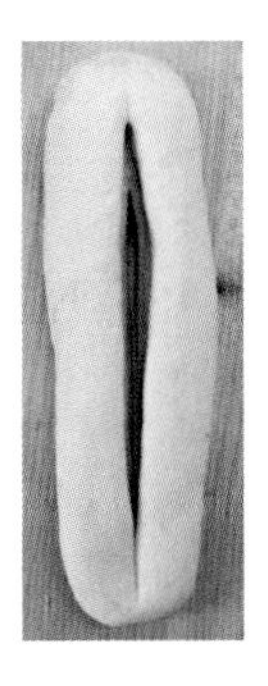

TSOUREKI

- 1½ cups milk (whole or 2%), lukewarm
- 2 packages active dry yeast
- 1½ teaspoons salt
- ½ cup butter (1 stick) melted
- ¾ cup sugar
- Zest and juice of one medium orange
- 2 teaspoons ground anise seed
- 5 large eggs, room temperature, lightly beaten
- 6 to 6½ cups all-purpose flour (plus more for kneading)
- Egg wash (1 egg beaten with 1 tablespoon of water)
- Sliced or slivered almonds

Combine milk, butter, sugar, and salt, and heat until sugar is dissolved and butter is melted; cool to lukewarm. In a large mixing bowl, dissolve yeast in milk mixture and add eggs, orange zest, and ground anise. Add five cups of flour, one cup at a time, mixing each time until flour is thoroughly incorporated. Let dough rest for 10 minutes before turning out onto a lightly floured board. Knead the dough as you add the remaining flour about ¼ cup at a time, until you get a soft dough that is smooth and elastic (about 5 minutes). Wash and dry the mixing bowl, lightly oil the surface of the dough, and place it back in the bowl. Cover with a dry dish towel and let rise in a warm place free from drafts for 60 to 90 minutes.

Punch dough down and knead briefly to expel larger air bubbles. Let dough rest 10 minutes. Lightly grease two large (12" x 18") jelly roll pan. Divide dough in half. Divide one portion into three pieces and roll each piece into a rope about 16 inches long. Braid the three ropes together and place on the pan. Repeat with second portion of dough. Cover with a clean, dry cloth and let rise for 45 to 60 minutes, or until nearly doubled. Preheat oven to 350°F.

Brush the surface of the loaf with the egg wash using a soft pastry brush, and sprinkle with almonds. Bake for 35 to 45 minutes. If the surface of the dough starts to brown too quickly, cover it loosely with foil for the last 15 minutes of baking.

The loaf is fully baked when an inserted cake tester comes out clean and the crust is a deep, rich brown—the interior temperature should be between 190°F and 195°F. Leave on the pans for 15 minutes, then transfer to a wire rack to cool. Makes two large loaves, 15 to 20 servings.

BREADHEAD BACK STORY

Tsoureki is a traditional Greek Easter bread, usually rich, braided, and accented with dyed eggs. The deep red eggs are meant to represent the blood of Christ, and many Greeks consider them an essential part of the bread. But my enthusiasm for this tradition has been dampened ever since I watched a fellow monk cut a slice THROUGH one of the eggs because he wanted a smaller portion, leaving bits of shell all over the table and in the remainder of the loaf. Besides, we get more than enough hard-boiled eggs during Easter week.

You might find it unusual that as a monk I'm not a staunch defender of culinary tradition, and in the case of Tsoureki I take any number of liberties. The traditional flavorings for this Greek treat are mastic (a spice made from resin which is dried and then ground) and aromatic mahlab (made from ground seeds of a cherry native to Greece). If you want a really traditional version of this recipe, you can easily find it online.

My version of this sweet, rich bread uses orange and anise as flavorings. I omit the red eggs, but there are plenty in the dough—five, to be exact, and one more used as a glaze. It also has a whole stick of butter and 3/4 cup of sugar, so it's a very rich dough. The dough is a bit sticky even after kneading, but resist the temptation to add more flour; things will get better after the first rise.

CINNAMON APPLE LATTICE BRAID

- 1 batch of Sour Cream Sweet Dough (see page 86)
- Cinnamon Apple Filling (see below)
- 1 egg beaten with 1 tablespoon of water for egg wash (optional)

Cinnamon Apple Filling

- 2 tablespoons of unsalted butter
- 5 cups tart apples; peeled, cored, and sliced (¼-inch thick)
- ½ cup granulated sugar
- ¼ cup brown sugar
- 1 tablespoon lemon juice
- 1½ teaspoons ground cinnamon
- 2 tablespoons cornstarch
- 2 tablespoons of water
- 1 teaspoon vanilla extract

Make the filling before you start the dough, so it can cool completely. You can even make it the day before and refrigerate, but take it out of the fridge while the dough is proofing to bring it to room temp (I usually transfer it to a new bowl that isn't cold).

After the dough has doubled for its first proof, punch it down gently and knead lightly to expel larger air bubbles. Cover with a clean, dry cloth and let rest 10 minutes to allow the gluten strands to relax so it will be easier to roll out. On a lightly floured board, roll out to a rectangle about 10 inches wide x 14 inches tall. Spread filling lengthwise in the center third of the dough, leaving a 1-inch edge of uncovered dough at top and bottom.

Using a sharp knife or a small pizza cutter, cut each outer third of the dough (the part not covered by the filling) into 5 to 10 diagonal strips, cutting from the edge of the dough to about 1 inch from the edge of the filling (see photos). Lightly brush strips with water. Fold strips over filling, alternating left and right, being careful not to stretch the dough. Tuck in the ends of the last strips and pinch to seal. Carefully transfer to a lightly greased baking pan. Cover and let rise in a warm, draft-free place for 30 minutes or until doubled.

If desired, brush surface of loaf with egg wash. Bake in a preheated 375°F. oven on the middle shelf for 30 minutes or until golden brown. Allow the loaf to

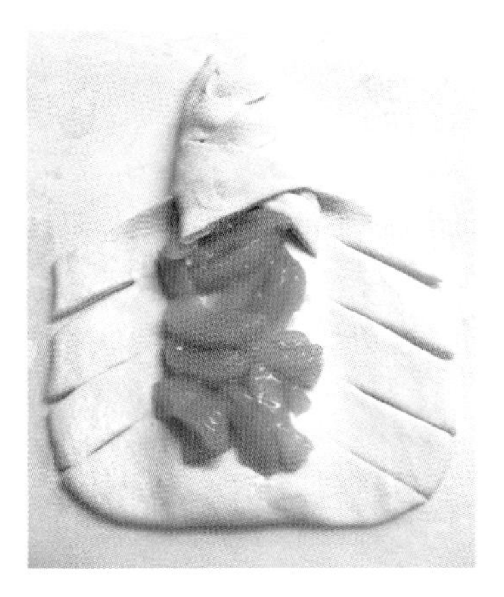

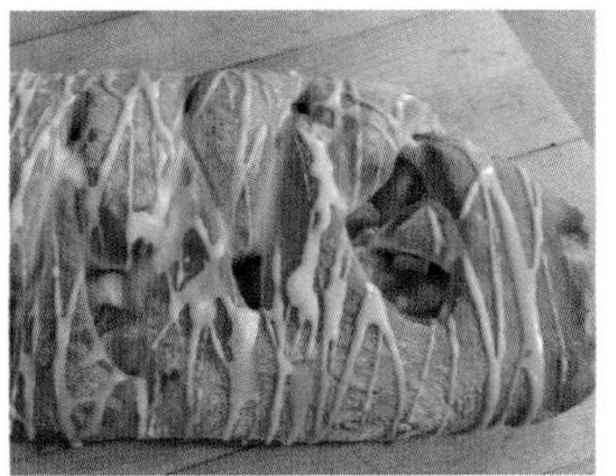

cool on the pan for 10 minutes before removing to a wire rack to cool to lukewarm, then decorate with powdered sugar drizzle (see page 130).

Filling

Melt butter in a 12-inch skillet and add apples, sugars, lemon juice, and cinnamon and stir to coat. Cook over medium heat, stirring regularly, until the apples are softened, and the sugar is dissolved, about 10 minutes. In a small bowl, whisk together cornstarch and water to make a runny paste. Add to the apple mixture along with the vanilla extract and cook, stirring gently but constantly, until the liquid is thickened and coats the apples, or until your family comes into the kitchen to find out what smells so good. Cool to room temperature before using.

NOTES

- I used apple filling in my pledge special video *Breakfast with the Bread Monk* but you can use any flavor of filling you like, about the same amount for a 9-inch pie. Fresh fruits are best, of course, but use canned pie filling in a pinch, or preserves.
- I published a similar recipe in a previous cookbook (*How to Be a Breadhead*) but that version used whole wheat dough and a savory filling of ham and cheese. But the technique works just as well for sweet breakfast breads. I have taught this shaping method to every level of baker, including junior high and high school students, and the results have always been spectacular. Just make sure you don't roll the dough out too wide (use a ruler to check the dimensions) and you should do just fine.

FABS' NUTTY GOODNESS ROLLS

Dough

1½ cups sour cream
2 tablespoons vegetable oil
½ cup sugar
2 packages yeast
½ cup water
¼ teaspoon soda
2 teaspoons salt
2 large eggs
4½ cups flour

Filling

⅓ cup packed brown sugar
⅓ cup granulated sugar
¼ cup all-purpose flour
1 tablespoon ground cinnamon
¼ cup (½ stick) cold butter, cut into ½-inch slices
½ cup chopped pecans

Note: This recipe appears in three of my other cookbooks, but it's my publisher's favorite breakfast bread and so he insisted I include it!

In a small bowl, proof yeast in the water. Warm sour cream, shortening, and sugar in a saucepan over medium heat—do not boil. Remove from heat and cool to lukewarm. Stir in soda and salt, then cool to lukewarm. Pour into large bowl, and add yeast and eggs, stirring until smooth. Add flour, about 1 cup at a time. Turn out onto lightly floured board and knead for about 3 minutes. Dough will be quite sticky, but avoid the temptation to add too much more flour, just a tablespoon or two to keep the dough manageable. Allow dough to rest for about 10 minutes (it will firm up nicely during this time.) In a small bowl, prepare filling by combining brown sugar, granulated sugar, flour, cinnamon, and butter; blend together with a pastry mixer or two knives until the mixture resembles coarse crumbs. Stir in the ½ cup of pecans. Prepare Caramel Sauce as directed. Roll dough out into a 18" x 16" rectangle. Sprinkle with filling. Roll up from long side, jelly roll style, and pinch to seal the edge (brush the edge with a little water if necessary to make it stick). Pour caramel sauce into the bottom of a lightly greased 9" x 13" x 2" pan, and sprinkle with the remaining ¾ cup of nuts. Cut dough crosswise into 12 rolls and place, cut side down, into the prepared pan. Cover and let rise for 45 to 60 minutes, or until nearly doubled. Place pan on a jelly roll pan to catch drips, and bake in a preheated 375°F. oven for 30 to 35 minutes. Invert onto serving plate while still warm.

Nutty Goodness Caramel Sauce
Combine ½ cup (1 stick) butter, 1 cup brown sugar, and ¼ cup corn syrup in a small sauce pan, and cook over medium heat just until sugar is dissolved. Remove from heat and cool slightly. Pour into pan and sprinkle on ¾ cup of chopped pecans.

NOTES

- I cannot make these rolls often enough for my students. Once when I was mixing the filling, one of the alumni, Jason "Fabs" Fabish, looked at the bowl of sugar and butter and nuts for the filling and exclaimed in a whisper, "Ohhhhhhhh—nutty goodness!" We have called them "Fabs' Nutty Goodness" ever since.

CHEESE BAPS

- 1½ cups lukewarm water (100°F to 110°F)
- 1 package active dry yeast
- 1 teaspoon sugar
- 3½ to 4 cups all-purpose flour, divided
- 1½ teaspoons salt
- 1 cup shredded sharp cheddar cheese
- Milk and flour for topping

In a medium-size bowl, sprinkle yeast, sugar, and ½ cup flour into lukewarm water and stir until thoroughly dissolved. Allow yeast to develop for 5 minutes. Stir in the salt. Add three cups of flour, one cup at a time, mixing after each addition until the flour is completely incorporated. Stir in cheese and mix thoroughly. About 2 tablespoons at a time, knead in enough of the remaining flour to make a soft, slightly sticky dough. Knead for 6 to 10 minutes, until dough is smooth and satiny. Lightly oil the surface of the dough and place it back into rinsed bowl and cover with a clean, dry towel. Allow to rise in a warm place free from drafts until doubled, about 60 minutes. Turn dough out of

bowl and knead gently to remove larger air bubbles. Divide dough into 8 to 12 pieces and shape each piece into a slightly flattened oval.

Place ovals on a lightly greased baking sheet, spacing them as far apart as possible—you may need two pans. Cover and let rise for about 30 minutes or until almost doubled in volume. Just before placing in oven, brush each oval lightly with milk and sprinkle heavily with flour. With a floured finger, make a deep impression in the center of each bap. Bake in a preheated 425°F oven for 15 to 20 minutes or until golden brown. Cool slightly on a wire rack; cover them with a light dish cloth as they cool to keep them soft.

NOTES

- Baps are a traditional breakfast bread in Scotland, where they are sliced lengthwise and filled with a fried egg and a couple of strips of bacon, or used for a sausage sandwich. In the Scottish countryside, it was common to wrap such a sandwich in waxed paper and tuck it in a jacket pocket to enjoy on the morning walk in the hills with your dog. Commuters would (and still do) grab one on the way out the door for breakfast on the train. For a slightly less messy sandwich, chop the bacon and use it for filling for a one-egg omelet—just the right size for this bun.

- This is a non-traditional recipe in that it has no milk or lard in the dough but instead uses cheese for flavor and texture. Scotland produces some mighty cheddars, so that's what I chose. Try pepper jack cheese for a spicier version; the resulting rolls would be enjoyed by anyone who puts Tabasco sauce on scrambled eggs.

LOUKOMADES

- 1 package of active dry yeast
- 1 teaspoon granulated sugar
- 1½ cups warm water
- ½ teaspoon salt
- 1 tablespoon vegetable oil
- 1 egg
- 1 teaspoon almond extract
- 3 cups all-purpose flour
- 2 cups honey
- ¼ cup water
- Ground cinnamon for sprinkling
- Chopped nuts (optional)
- Vegetable oil for frying

In a medium-size bowl, dissolve yeast and sugar in the warm water and let stand for about 5 minutes. Stir in salt and oil. Add the egg and almond extract; beat until blended. Add the flour, one cup at a time, stirring after each addition until flour is thoroughly incorporated and the mixture is smooth. Beat for one minute more, then cover the bowl with plastic wrap and let rise for 90 minutes in a warm place.

Heat oil to 375°F; there should be at least two inches of oil in the pot. Do not stir batter down. Use a tablespoon to drop tablespoons of batter into the oil (if you dip the spoon into the oil first, the batter will slide off easily). Fry only a few loukomades at a time; do not crowd the pot. Fry the fritters until they are golden brown on all sides, 3 or 4 minutes. Remove with a slotted spoon or tongs and drain on paper towels.

Warm honey with ¼ cup of water in a sauce pan over medium heat. Dip fritters in honey and roll in nuts if desired. Sprinkle with cinnamon and serve warm.

NOTES

- These Greek fritters are easy to prepare and truly exquisite: light and crisp, with a tender center. The batter mixes up in five minutes, rises for an hour and a half; then you fry them up. The traditional way to serve them is to coat them in honey and sprinkle on cinnamon. You can serve them warm, but many people claim that they are best after the honey has soaked in for a few hours. Loukomades are excellent anyway you serve them.

COOKIES & BARS

I come from a cookie-baking family, and there are a number of excellent recipes here, but Banana Coconut Cookies are my absolute favorite. Even people who say they normally don't like coconut *love* these cookies. Readers may be mystified that I don't have any cake recipes, nor any for brownies. Let's just say that I have never made a cake that was worthy of a photograph, and I haven't found a brownie recipe that was substantially better than a brand name box mix. Plus, I almost always over bake both! Cookies, however, I can manage.

BANANA COCONUT COOKIES

- 2½ cups all-purpose flour
- 1 cup (2 packages) instant banana pudding mix
- 1 teaspoon baking powder
- ½ teaspoon baking soda
- ½ teaspoon salt
- 1 cup (2 sticks) margarine
- 1½ cups granulated sugar
- 2 eggs
- ¼ cup milk
- 1 teaspoon banana extract
- 1½ teaspoons vanilla extract
- 1 cup sweetened shredded coconut

In a medium-size bowl, combine flour, pudding mix, baking powder, baking soda, and salt, and whisk blend completely. In another bowl or stand mixer, cream together margarine and sugar until light and fluffy. Add eggs, milk, and extracts and beat until well blended. Add flour mixture and mix well. Stir in coconut until evenly distributed throughout dough. Wrap dough in waxed paper or plastic wrap and chill in refrigerator for at least two hours.

Preheat oven to 375°F. Drop balls of chilled dough the size of walnuts on lightly greased baking sheets (you can line the pans with parchment paper instead) and flatten balls slightly. Bake for 10 minutes or until browned. Yields about 4 dozen cookies. See photo on page 106.

BREADHEAD BACK STORY

Every year since I joined the monastery, my mother would make these cookies and ship them to me for my birthday. In 2017, she suffered a stroke on my birthday. When I visited her in the hospital, one of the first things she told me was that she was sorry she didn't get the cookies baked. It was typical of her to think about her children before herself. Sadly, she died a few days later. Shortly after the funeral, I was on the phone with my mother's cousin and told her how Mom had been concerned that I didn't get my birthday cookies. She told me that my mother had sent Banana Coconut Cookies some to her a few weeks earlier and that she still had some in the freezer. She mailed them to me, and they were the best tasting batch of cookies I ever had, tears and all.

DRIED CHERRY BISCOTTI

- 2 cups flour
- 2 teaspoons baking powder
- ⅛ teaspoon salt
- 1 cup dried cherries
- ¾ cup white baking chips (regular or mini)
- 3 large eggs
- ¾ cup granulated sugar
- 1 teaspoon vanilla extract

Preheat oven to 350°F. Place flour, baking powder, and salt in a medium-size mixing bowl and whisk thoroughly until combined. Stir in cherries and baking chips. In a separate bowl, beat eggs, sugar, and vanilla extract until smooth. Add the egg mixture to the dry ingredients and mix well. Turn the dough out onto a lightly floured work surface and knead briefly.

Shape the dough into a log about 12 inches long and 4 inches wide and place it on a parchment lined baking sheet. Bake for about 30 minutes, or until golden brown and firm to the touch. Remove from the oven and cool on a wire rack for 30 minutes.

Transfer the dough to a cutting board and slice the log into ½-inch slices. Place the slices back on the baking sheet, cut side down, and bake at 325°F for 7 minutes. Turn the slices over and bake for an additional 7 minutes. Remove from oven and cool completely.

NOTES

- Biscotti (literally "twice baked") are an Italian cookie originating in Prato and traditionally made with almonds. Chocolate and anise versions are also popular.
- I was inspired to make these when some friends of mine brought me back dried cherries from Michigan. The combination of tart and sweet is delicious. You can substitute dried cranberries if you prefer.
- Many biscotti recipes call to dip them in melted chocolate or almond bark, but resist the temptation with this recipe—these are plenty sweet as is!

BLONDIES

- 1 cup (2 sticks) butter
- 2 cups packed light brown sugar
- 2 large eggs
- 2 teaspoons vanilla extract
- 2 cups all-purpose flour
- 1 teaspoon baking powder
- ½ teaspoon salt
- 1 cup chopped walnuts (optional)

Preheat oven to 350°F and spray an 8" x 8" pan with cooking spray. In a medium-size bowl or in the stand mixer, place flour, baking powder, and salt and whisk until thoroughly combined. Set aside. In a fairly large sauce pan, melt the butter and then stir in the brown sugar while the pan is still warm, until thoroughly combined. Cool to lukewarm and add in the eggs and vanilla extract, then whisk vigorously until smooth. Add the butter mixture to the dry ingredients and beat until smooth. Fold in the nuts if desired. Pour the batter into the prepared pan and smooth out the top with a rubber spatula. Place in the oven to bake for 30 minutes until edges are golden and an inserted toothpick comes out fairly clean. Allow to cool completely, then cut into squares: 9 for hearty servings, 12 to 16 for more modest portions!

NOTES

- I really love blondies, but I have to say I much prefer them with walnuts over anything else, as do my fellow monks. But you will also see recipes using pecans, butterscotch chips, or chocolate chips. Try several versions and see which your family likes best.
- If you don't have an 8" x 8" pan you can also bake these in a 9" x 13" pan for 25 minutes.

BUTTERSCOTCH GINGERBREAD COOKIES

- 1 cup shortening
- 1 cup brown sugar
- 2 eggs
- 3 cups cake flour
- 2 (3.4 ounce) boxes of instant butterscotch pudding
- 3 teaspoons ground ginger
- 1 teaspoon cinnamon
- ¼ teaspoon nutmeg
- 1 teaspoon baking soda

Cream together shortening and brown sugar until light and fluffy—this is easiest in a stand mixer, but you can do it by hand if you have the patience and the arm strength! Add eggs and beat until smooth. In a separate bowl, combine flour, pudding mix, spices, and baking soda, and whisk until thoroughly blended. Add dry ingredients to the liquid and mix well. Wrap dough in waxed paper and chill for at least one hour. On a lightly floured board, roll dough out to ¼-inch thickness and cut out cookies with your favorite cutters. Place on a lightly greased cookie sheet and bake in a preheated oven at 350°F for 8 to10 minutes or until slightly browned. Let cool on the pan for five minutes before transferring to a wire rack to cool completely.

NOTES

- If you enjoy spiced cookies but are not a fan of the molasses in gingerbread, these cookies are for you. Warm from the oven with cold milk, these butterscotch gingerbread cutouts are completely irresistible. That's why the recipe makes a big batch—you may eat as many as you store!
- You can use whatever cutters you like, but I prefer teddy bears—the shape seems to go well with the color of the dough. Be careful not to overbake, as these cookies do not brown at the edges as much as some sugar cookie recipes. They'll be a little soft when you remove them from the oven but harden up nicely as they cool.

COWBOY COOKIES

- 2 cups all-purpose flour
- 1 teaspoon baking soda
- ½ teaspoon baking powder
- ½ teaspoon salt
- 1 cup shortening
- 1 cup granulated sugar
- 1 cup brown sugar, firmly packed
- 2 eggs
- 1 teaspoon vanilla extract
- 2 cups old-fashioned rolled oats
- 1 cup (6 ounces) semi-sweet chocolate morsels

Preheat oven to 350°F. In a medium-size bowl, sift together flour, baking soda, baking powder, and salt and whisk to combine. Set aside.

Cream together shortening and sugars, then beat in eggs and vanilla extract until light and fluffy. Stir in the flour mixture until well blended. Add rolled oats and chocolate chips and stir until evenly distributed.

Drop by teaspoonfuls onto a lightly greased cookie sheet and bake at 350°F for 15 minutes or until lightly browned.

BREADHEAD BACK STORY

As we were cleaning out the house after my mother's death, we of course came across a thousand memories a day, many of them in the kitchen. On the top shelf of the kitchen cabinet we found the coffee can, decorated in classic '70s style, in which she kept her chocolate chips and coconut, clearly labeled "For Cookies." I used to sneak chocolate chips, but I should have known my mother would discover the culprit. One day I opened the canister to discover a note (addressing me by my baptismal name) that stated emphatically: "Michael, if you eat any more of these chocolate chips I will break your arm!" My siblings made sure I got the canister and its contents after the funeral. In addition to a bag of milk chocolate chips, it held a note that read: "Dom, enjoy the chocolate. No broken arms—your sibs."

FOR COOKIES

CANDY SHOP

Just a few more sweet treats. I've yet to be successful at making a decent chewy caramel, but everyone loves my caramel corn and wants the recipe. Our Fr. Michael shared his grandmother's fudge recipe, and I found a recipe card in my mom's file for candied pecans that she used to make as a special treat when I was home from the monastery.

GRANDMA WERNSTRUM'S FUDGE

- 4 cups granulated sugar
- 1 cup (2 sticks) butter
- 1 cup evaporated milk
- 1 teaspoon vanilla extract
- 2 cups semi-sweet chocolate chips
- 2 cups milk chocolate chips
- 2 ounces bitter chocolate, chopped
- 25 large marshmallows
- 1½ cups chopped walnuts (optional)

Butter a 9" x 13" baking pan (not a cookie sheet) and set aside. In a large saucepan, combine sugar, butter, and evaporated milk over medium heat and bring to a slow boil. Boil for two minutes or until sugar is completely dissolved, stirring constantly. Reduce heat to low. Stir in the vanilla extract, then add marshmallows five at a time, letting them melt most of the way before adding more. When the marshmallows are completely dissolved, add the two kinds of chocolate chips and the chopped bittersweet chocolate. Stir vigorously until the mixture becomes smooth and glossy. Stir in walnuts if desired. Pour mixture in the prepared pan and smooth the top. Allow to cool for several hours before cutting into small squares.

NOTES

- Our Fr. Michael and I used to make this recipe every year at Christmas, but we started getting so many other treats from family and friends that we decided to make this into a treat for Epiphany or even Valentine's Day.
- When I say "large marshmallows" I mean to distinguish them from mini-marshmallows, not the "jumbo" ones that are available now. My recommendations to expedite matters by using mini-marshmallows or marshmallow crème were met with polite but firm refusal from Fr. Michael, traditionalist that he is: "We're doing it like Grandma did!"
- Be advised that you may want to have a partner for stirring, so you can switch off. Grandma Wernstrum must have had forearms like Popeye! We've found that a heavy-sided pot helps retain the heat of the mixture as you stir in the marshmallows.
- I much prefer fudge with nuts, and toasted walnuts are best in my opinion—not sure what Grandma Wernstrum would have said about that.

LOUISIANA CANDIED PECANS

½ cup (1 stick) unsalted butter
2 egg whites
1 cup granulated sugar
1 teaspoon salt
½ teaspoon vanilla extract
1 pound pecan halves

Place butter on a 9" x 13" baking sheet (with sides, not a flat cookie sheet) and place in the oven. Turn the oven to 350° F. Beat whites until soft peaks form, then continue whisking while gradually adding sugar, salt and vanilla. Beat until the mixture turns thick and glossy. Fold in the nuts until well coated and evenly distributed. Remove pan from oven and spread nut mixture evenly over the melted butter in the pan. Bake 30 minutes, stirring and turning the nuts with a spatula every 8 minutes or so, until there is no longer any butter in the pan. Remove nuts from the pan and place them on foil or parchment and allow to cool completely before storing in an airtight container.

NOTES

- This recipe is another from my mother's recipe cards, written in her own hand with characteristically brief instructions. I have expanded the directions somewhat, but these still taste like the ones used to make once in a great while as a special treat—pecans are expensive!
- I have also seen these called Swedish nuts. You can make them with walnuts if you prefer. Some people add ½ teaspoon of cinnamon to the sugar, but I prefer not to mask the flavor of the roasted pecans.

SALTED BUTTER TOFFEE CARAMEL CORN

Equipment Needed

8 to 10 quart pan with an oven-safe handle

Medium saucepan

Candy thermometer

Heavy wooden spoon

Two 9" x 13" cookie sheets

4 quarts of popped popcorn (sort out the unpopped kernels)

1 stick (½ cup) of butter (not margarine or spread)

1 cup light brown sugar

¼ cup corn syrup (not the low calorie)

1 teaspoon vanilla extract

Popcorn salt (optional)

Preheat oven to 300°F. Place the popcorn in an 8 to 10 quart metal pot or pan with an oven-safe handle (you may want to lightly spray the interior of pan with pan release first) and warm in the oven. Place butter, brown sugar, corn syrup, and vanilla extract in a small saucepan over medium heat, stirring constantly, until ingredients are melted and well mixed. Clip the candy thermometer on the side of the pan so that the tip touches the mixture but not the bottom of the pan. Keep stirring the mixture occasionally. When the caramel temperature reaches about 250°F, take the popcorn pan out of the oven and have it nearby on the counter along with an oven mitt to hold the hot pan. When the caramel temperature reaches 300°F, turn off the heat, remove the thermometer, and pour the caramel onto the popcorn. Using a large and heavy wooden spoon, stir the caramel into the popcorn until the corn is evenly coated. (You may have to put the pan back in the oven to re-melt the caramel if you don't work quickly enough.) Divide the caramel corn between the two baking sheets and spread it out flat. Sprinkle lightly with popcorn salt if desired (the salty/sweet combination is excellent!). Let cool until hard, then break apart gently and store in an airtight container.

NOTES

- I make a lot of caramel corn, usually using popcorn leftover from the concession stand during the basketball season. So although most recipes call for unbuttered, unsalted popcorn, you can use just about anything that isn't stale. Also, most caramel corn recipes instruct you to mix the caramel with the popcorn and then put it in a roasting pan in the oven, stirring it every 10 or 15 minutes for up to an hour. As far as I can tell, the purpose of this oven step is to re-melt the caramel so that you can get it to coat the popcorn evenly. I have learned through much experimentation that the better method is to get a large (8 to 10 quart) metal pan or pot with an oven-safe handle in which to put the popcorn, and preheat both the popcorn and the pan while you are making the caramel. When the caramel goes on the corn in the pan, it doesn't lose heat as quickly, and you can often get a batch made in a single mixing. If you are used to the oven method, try this at least once and tell me what you think.

TOPPINGS & SPREADS

Everyone has a favorite flavor of jam or jelly, but apple butter made from the fruit in our monastery orchard is a special treat. Your scones and cinnamon rolls will need some kind of icing, too, and compound butters are a quick but flavorful complement to just about any baked good.

COMPOUND BUTTERS

Compound butters are simply mixtures of butter with other ingredients or flavorings. They can be sweet or savory, and are used to enhance the flavor of everything from morning toast to midnight snack and everything in between. Many savory compound butters are used as a topping for steak, including such French classics as such as *beurre à la bourguignonne* (garlic and parsley butter) or *beurre Maitre d'Hotel* (butter with parsley and lemon juice). I've been making savory herb butters for years using the fruits of our labors in the abbey garden and apiary, but I decided to expand my repertoire into sweet butters for this book. See photo on page 124.

Note: For savory butters involving herbs, garlic, and cheeses, I use salted butter. For sweet butters, I recommend using unsalted butter and adding just a pinch of salt to enhance the flavors.

Raspberry Walnut Butter

1 stick unsalted butter, softened

¼ cup raspberries

1 tablespoon honey or more to taste

¼ cup toasted walnuts, chopped

Fresh raspberries are generally available almost year round, and their sweetness varies greatly, so you may need more honey than a single tablespoon. This butter is a tasty way to dress up a healthy multigrain bread, and it has so much flavor you don't need to slather it on too thick.

Brown Sugar Spice Butter

1 stick unsalted butter, softened

2 tablespoons brown sugar

½ teaspoon vanilla extract

½ teaspoon Chinese Five Spice

Be sure you make this well in advance, so the brown sugar can dissolve completely in the butter, best achieved with an electric mixer or small food-processor. The Chinese Five Spice usually includes fennel and star anise, along with cinnamon, pepper, and cloves, so it has a spicy flavor with licorice overtones. It's especially delicious on a toasted English muffin.

Cranberry Citrus Butter

1 cup fresh cranberries

2 sticks unsalted butter, softened

Zest and juice of half a medium orange or lime

¼ cup chopped toasted pecans

honey to taste

This butter has a flavor profile similar to the classic fresh cranberry salad, although using lime instead of orange gives it a deliciously tart twist. Try this on a plain dinner roll or croissant.

Honey Coriander Butter

1 stick unsalted butter

¼ cup honey

1 teaspoon ground coriander

A good introduction to coriander, the seed of the cilantro plant but with a very different flavor: spicy with a citrusy undertone. I love this on top of cornbread or Irish soda bread.

Honey Sriracha Butter

1 stick unsalted butter, softened

1 tablespoon honey

1 teaspoon Sriracha

Pinch of salt

Sweet and hot is an increasingly popular flavor combination, and this butter is an easy way to add it to your culinary experimentation. Spread this over toast and top it with a poached egg. You can add more Sriracha to taste, and consider adding a little lime or lemon zest for another layer of flavor to accompany corn on the cob (not really a breakfast food, but you'll have some leftover!).

APPLE BUTTER

Equipment Needed

1 wide 12-quart stock pot (Stainless steel with a heavy bottom is best)

A food mill

8 pounds of apples

1 cup apple cider vinegar

2 cups water

Brown sugar (up to 4 cups)

½ teaspoon salt

2 teaspoons cinnamon

1 teaspoon allspice

Cut the apples into quarters—no need to peel or core them, but cut out any parts that are badly bruised, bird marked, or damaged by pests. (Red peels, by the way, give the apple butter a lovely color.)

Put apples into the pot, then add the vinegar and water. Cover and bring to a boil, then reduce heat to a simmer and cook uncovered until the apples are soft, about 30 minutes. Remove from heat and stir with a heavy spoon until you have a thick, lumpy purée. Remove from heat and cool slightly.

Ladle the purée into a food mill in small batches and process. Stir in salt, cinnamon, and allspice. Add 2 cups of sugar and stir to dissolve. Taste—add more sugar in small amounts as needed. Too much sugar and you lose the taste of the apples, too little and the apple cider becomes the dominant flavor.

Return pot to the stove and cook uncovered on medium-low heat, stirring constantly to prevent scorching. Be sure to scrape the bottom of the pot while you stir, so the sugar doesn't form a crust and burn. Cook until the apple butter is thick and smooth (about 4 to 6 hours). If you spoon some onto a chilled white plate, there should be no liquid run-off.

APRICOT CHUTNEY

- 1 30-ounce can of apricot halves in heavy syrup
- 2 cups golden raisins
- ½ cup freshly minced onion
- 1 or 2 tablespoons balsamic vinegar
- ½ teaspoon powdered ginger
- ¼ teaspoon crushed red pepper
- ¼ teaspoon ground cumin
- Pinch of ground cloves

Remove apricot halves from syrup and coarsely chop them. Place chopped apricots, about half the heavy syrup, and the raisins and onion into a medium-size saucepan and bring to a simmer over medium-high heat, stirring constantly. (Discard remaining syrup.) Add remaining ingredients and mix well. Reduce heat to low and simmer 15 minutes or until thickened, stirring occasionally.

BREADHEAD BACK STORY

Chutney is a staple of the cuisine of India and Nepal, where it is a side dish or dipping sauce which can be made of everything from tomatoes to cucumbers and yogurt to ground peanuts. It was brought back to Great Britain where it became a spicy/sweet/tart amalgam of fruit, spices, sugar, and vinegar.

The first time I had apricot chutney was in an upscale sandwich shop, where it was mixed with whipped cream cheese and spread over deli-sliced turkey on wheat bread. I fell in love immediately and having developed this recipe I make it regularly. You can certainly make this scrumptious chutney with fresh apricots, but their season is limited, so I use canned fruit most often. Using fruit in heavy syrup means there is no need to add sugar, but you can use apricots in clear juice and add apricot nectar or honey for additional sweetness to taste. Excellent on top of toasted bagels or Belgian waffles, too.

GLAZE, DRIZZLE, & FROSTING

So what's the difference? Glaze is a thin layer of icing (think glazed donuts) that is translucent. Drizzle is a thin stream of pourable icing swirled on top of scones, coffeecakes, and some rolls. Frosting is a creamy, spreadable topping using butter, cream cheese, or both, along with powdered sugar.

Donut Glaze

(Makes enough for a dozen donuts)

¼ cup milk (2% OK, whole milk if you have it)

1 teaspoon vanilla extract

2 cups powdered sugar

Place milk in a medium-size microwave safe bowl and heat for 15 seconds or until warm. Stir in the vanilla extract. Sift the powdered sugar into milk mixture and whisk until well combined. Dip doughnuts into the glaze, one at a time, and set on a wire rack with waxed paper or a pan underneath. Rewarm the glaze as needed to get a thin coating. Wait 5 to 10 minutes for the glaze to firm up before serving.

Drizzle

(Makes enough for a batch of scones)

½ cup powdered sugar

2 or 3 teaspoons of milk/cream

¼ teaspoon vanilla or almond extract

Pinch of salt

Combine all ingredients in a microwave safe glass pitcher and stir until smooth. Heat in microwave for 15 seconds and stir again. Use the pitcher to pour the drizzle in swirls or other decorative patterns.

Frosting

3 cups powdered sugar

½ cup (1 stick) room temperature butter (I prefer salted)

2 teaspoons vanilla extract, use clear extract to prevent discoloration

2–3 tablespoons heavy cream

In a medium-size mixing bowl, add powdered sugar, butter, vanilla extract, and milk and mix until smooth and creamy.

Pour over warm rolls and spread. Some of the glaze with get absorbed and some of it will set on top. Enjoy!

NOTES

- One of my favorite ways to make a special drizzle is to use flavored half-and-half for the liquid. Think of possibilities: French vanilla with apricot coffeecake, hazelnut with chocolate scones, Irish Cream on top of a Danish pastry filled with pear preserves, pumpkin spice on baked donuts.
- As a general rule I prefer light drizzle on my breakfast breads rather than full-on frosting, as I think the latter tends to dominate the flavors too much. However, there is something to be said for the occasional decadent, over-the-top, frosted cinnamon roll!

INDEX